D1807218

The Tournament
and Literature

Studies in the Humanities
Literature—Politics—Society

Guy Mermier
General Editor

Vol. 49

PETER LANG
New York • Washington, D.C./Baltimore • Boston • Bern
Frankfurt am Main • Berlin • Brussels • Vienna • Canterbury

Mary Arlene Santina

The Tournament and Literature

Literary Representations of the Medieval Tournament in Old French Works, 1150–1226

PETER LANG
New York • Washington, D.C./Baltimore • Boston • Bern
Frankfurt am Main • Berlin • Brussels • Vienna • Canterbury

Library of Congress Cataloging-in-Publication Data

Santina, Mary Arlene.
The tournament and literature: literary representations of the medieval
tournament in Old French works, 1150–1226 / Mary Arlene Santina.
p. cm. — (Studies in the humanities; vol. 49)
Includes bibliographical references and index.
1. French literature—To 1500—History and criticism. 2. Tournaments,
Medieval, in literature. 3. Knights and knighthood in literature.
4. Civilization, Medieval, in literature. 5. Chivalry in
literature. I. Title. II. Series: Studies in the
humanities (New York; N.Y.); vol. 49.
PQ158.S26   840.9'355—DC21   98-33748
ISBN 0-8204-4280-1
ISSN 0742-6712

Die Deutsche Bibliothek-CIP-Einheitsaufnahme

Santina, Mary Arlene:
The tournament and literature: literary representations of the medieval
tournament in old French works, 1150–1226 / Mary Arlene Santina.
–New York; Washington, D.C./Baltimore; Boston; Bern;
Frankfurt am Main; Berlin; Brussels; Vienna; Canterbury: Lang.
(Studies in the humanities; Vol. 49)
ISBN 0-8204-4280-1

The paper in this book meets the guidelines for permanence and durability
of the Committee on Production Guidelines for Book Longevity
of the Council of Library Resources.

© 1999 Peter Lang Publishing, Inc., New York

All rights reserved.
Reprint or reproduction, even partially, in all forms such as microfilm,
xerography, microfiche, microcard, and offset strictly prohibited.

Printed in the United States of America

Acknowledgments

I would like to thank greatly Professor Guy R. Mermier for his patience and anticipation of this work, as well as his recognition of the value of and need for it in the scholarly realm. Further thanks are due Professor Elizabeth Wilson Poe and Professor Catharine Savage Brosman for their helpful comments and encouragement. Many thanks go to Meg, Don, and Margaret for their unending enthusiasm, to Wendy and Vic for their deep interest, and to Jacqueline for her solid belief in my writing. Thank you P. W. Sheetz and M. M. Forté for your initial suggestions. Special thanks go to my father Henry and my sister Virginia. And lastly, but most of all, to my husband Peter Andronaco for everything, and without whom this could not have been achieved.

Preface

The majority of scholarly publications about the Medieval Tournament have been historical and seek to define the sport itself, concentrating on its origins and the various techniques involved. Whereas such works have provided scholars with useful information for an understanding of the tournament rules and procedures, in order to comprehend fully the phenomenon it is necessary to examine it from another perspective, one of a literary nature; hence the basis for this book.

The originality of the following endeavor from prior ones on the subject lies in that I review literary works in order to determine how the different aspects that compose the tournament are therein portrayed. How were the diverse elements of the sport utilized by the poets? The sport was incorporated into the narratives, no doubt in part, because of the integral part it played in the life of a knight but surely there were other purposes. The task at hand is to examine the diverse ways in which tournaments figure in Medieval French literature, and to see the tournament as both an historical and fictional topic. This is accomplished through schematic analysis rather than pure narrative, and the literature of the era provides the evidence and the sources for this task.

I have purposely paraphrased most of the long and potentially difficult passages from Old French while at the same time I have included the original versions, keeping some of the shorter verses in parentheses. Anticipating that Old French can be rather difficult to understand, I wanted this to be a publication that would be read and understood as easily by first-time acquaintances with the subject as it would be by experts and/or life-time medievalists. Mine is not to select and exclude readers, rather, I should hope that all who read this book will learn from it as well as develop an enthusiasm that will carry them onto further readings on the topic.

Table of Contents

Introduction

The tournament was one of the great social phenomena of a past, at that time modern, civilization. It had a significant impact on the daily life of the knight, as well as on contemporary literature inasmuch as descriptions of the tournament figure prominently in many literary works of the time. However, the tournament of such an early age as the twelfth century is consistently and unfortunately misunderstood in modern days. Such misunderstandings can in part be attributed to the masterpiece story, *Ivanhoe*,[1] by Sir Walter Scott in 1819 where in chapter VIII he describes a fanciful tournament, and perhaps more attributable to the delightfully illustrated *Traité de la forme et devis d'un tournoi* by René d'Anjou in the fifteenth century.[2]

In René's guide, there are beautifully colored pictures of knights in elegant finery, accompanied by their horses, also decorated and draped in bright cloaks. There are tents filled with numerous noble ladies and people. The knights furthermore, joust one-on-one and do not charge in large groups. René details how the challenge for a tournament is formally written down and couriered to an opponent who must accept the challenge or decline. These are images which render the tournament a romantic event to students, but whereas the descriptions are no doubt quite accurate, they are accurate for a certain time-frame in the life of the sport; these images are indicative of the game after it had been altered and carried into the fourteenth and fifteenth centuries. The sport at its inception was scarcely the same and differed to a great extent.

While this is not to be a book about the differences in the sport throughout the centuries, I leave that to the historians,[3] this is to be a book about the different ways the tournament and its components appear in the literature of the late twelfth century and the early thirteenth century; a book which in the process, reveals a tournament unlike the one commonly imagined. The role of the *tornoi*, or *turneiement*, in this medieval literature is as diverse as the early spellings of the word itself. It is represented throughout the literature in many different ways, playing many roles; for example, in a few works the authors attribute moral or even allegorical significance to it. In certain texts, long and detailed descriptions of the tournament create remarkable visual effects. One constant though, is that tourneying serves as an important gauge of a knight's reputation. These among other facets are what will comprise this book which the author hopes, will be a useful guide for those interested in the sport, as well as provide better insight into this fascinating manifestation of a long ago age.

Corpus of Works

Since several works used as sources for this book may not be familiar to the reader, I find it worthwhile and helpful to list in genres, as well as briefly describe, the selected material to which I will consistently refer. The works chosen are in Old French verse (hence a link with poetry), and date from 1150 to 1226. I am using these narratives (as they may also be called) because they were written within approximately one hundred years of the first French attestation of the term *turnei*. The cutoff year of 1226 is the accepted date of the only commissioned biographical work of this study.

Histoires
L'Histoire de Guillaume le Maréchal[4] is the story of William Marshal, an Englishman of relatively humble origins who, through his natural talents, became a well-known knight and a respected figure within the English and French royal courts. He initially became wealthy as a result of his successes in tournaments; later though, through his marriage to Isabelle de Clare, the daughter of the Earl of Pembroke, he acquired aristocratic standing, along with the new titles of Count of Striguil and of Pembroke. William was a tutor/companion to the young king Henry,[5] son of King Henry II of England. They remained good friends until the Young King's untimely death in 1183. William in turn knew and served two kings of England: namely, Richard I, the Lion-Heart and John Lackland. He also was well-acquainted with the French King, Philip II. After the death of King John in 1216, William was

chosen Regent of England for the child king, Henry III, remaining Regent until William's death three years later. The 19,215-verse narrative is comprehensive in its account of this interesting figure: it begins in the early years of the first marriage of his father, continues through William's birth, assumed to be 1144, and ends with his death in 1219. The *histoire* was commissioned by his oldest son, also named William Marshal, and most likely completed in 1226. The author's identity is still debated, although there is good evidence that it was the squire of William Marshal Sr., Jean d'Erlée.[6] D'Erlée at least contributed much of the material, even if he did not personally write it all down.[7] The story of William has proven to be an important source because it does exist in its entirety and it contains several thorough descriptions of tournaments in which William participated and found fame. In all, there are references to sixteen tournaments, either alluded to or described to some degree.

Lais

There are five *lais* by Marie de France, circa 1170: "Milun," "Guigemar," "Le Laüstic," "Le Fresne," and "Chaitivel."[8] The *lais* by Marie de France, are short, rhymed tales of love and intrigue that she drew from the so-called "matière de Bretagne." Guigemar is the hero of the *lai* of the same name, in whose 886 verses a tournament is announced, but never takes place. "Le Fresne" (518 verses), likewise, does not narrate a tournament, but Marie alludes to one for a specific reason; the same can be said for "Le Laüstic" (160 verses). "Milun" (534 verses) is a tale of love, but is more about a father's quest for his son. Milun, the hero, competes in a tournament, the importance of which will be explained later. The last *lai* by Marie to be treated, "Chaitivel" (240 verses), is framed around a tournament that constitutes the central scene of the story.

The anonymous *lai* "Doon,"[9] mid-to-late twelfth century, is composed of 288 verses and is similar to Marie's "Milun," in that the father, Doon, sets out on a quest to find his son. During this quest, Doon enters a tournament in Brittany where he encounters the son he has been seeking.

Another anonymous *lai* to which I will refer is entitled "Le Lecheor,"[10] circa twelfth century. It does not describe any tournaments but does refer to them in a unique manner. The principal characters in this piece are eight of the finest ladies of Brittany who, throughout 124 verses, have a remarkable discussion about knights and their pastimes.

Romans

Chrétien de Troyes, a contemporary of Marie de France, chose to write romances (*romans*) based on the Arthurian legend instead of *lais*. Of the five romances chosen, circa 1170–1190, all include a tournament, except for *Yvain, Le Chevalier au lion* (6825 verses),[11] which merely refers to one. The romance of *Erec et Enide* (6762 verses),[12] which begins shortly before the marriage of the two protagonists, recounts a series of adventures, several of which relate directly to the sport of tourneying. *Le Chevalier de la charrete* (7112 verses),[13] tells the story of Lancelot, the Knight of the Lake, and in particular, his love affair with Queen Guinevere. *Cligés* (6664 verses)[14] begins with a long section about the background and circumstances of the hero Cligés' birth in Constantinople. It continues with his journey to Britain and subsequent adventures before returning to his homeland where he eventually marries his love Fenice. *Le Conte du Graal*[15] was Chrétien's final romance and his longest, consisting of 8960 verses. It remains incomplete, presumably because Chrétien died before he could finish it. The tournament in question has nothing to do with Perceval, but instead involves the knight Sir Gawain.

Hue de Rotelande is the author of the 10,580-verse romance *Ipomedon*, circa 1180,[16] the story of a young prince, Ipomedon, who falls in love with a haughty princess, *la Fiere pucele*, and she with him. Ipomedon travels from his home in La Pouille, an old kingdom in the modern day region of Apulia, Italy, to the princess' realm of Calabria where he is to participate in the one tournament in the work; its description entails more than 2300 verses alone.

The anonymous romance *Partonopeus de Blois*, mid-to-late-twelfth century,[17] is composed of 10,856 verses, but unfortunately, the manuscript has a lacuna of eight pages or approximately 1040 verses.[18] This gap occurs just after the end of the first day of a three-day tournament and continues until shortly after the third day's competition has begun. The hero is Partonopeus and his love is Mélior.

The final romance, also by an anonymous author and written in the Picard french dialect, is entitled *Amadas et Ydoine*, late twelfth to early thirteenth century.[19] It is a 7912-verse story of two youngsters in love, the eponymous heroes. Amadas is the central figure of the story. He is a young knight who must overcome an illness, and who is able to regain his reputation for prowess by competing in a tournament. In all, in this romance there are two actual tournaments and two referred to in some manner.

Romans d'antiquité

There are two *romans d'antiquité* by anonymous authors, which I separate from the other romances because of their themes of classical antiquity. The story of *Enéas*[20] is a twelfth-century, circa 1155, French account, in 10,156 verses, of the siege of Troy, adapted from Virgil's *Aeneid*. The *Roman de Thèbes*[21] (10,562 verses) is a twelfth-century, circa 1163, French adaptation of the siege of Thebes, taken from that told by Statius. While neither *roman d'antiquité* is the story of a tournament, each is pertinent since the word *tornoi* is used by the authors to describe the sieges within and such usage of the term will be discussed.

Chroniques historiques

L'Estoire de la guerre sainte[22] by Ambroise, circa 1195, is an historical chronicle of the Third Holy War led by King Richard I of England. It is an extensive account, approximately 12,150 verses, of King Richard's crusade for Christianity. It begins well before his departure from Britain, including passages about his coronation in 1189. It ends with his homecoming in 1194, having briefly mentioned Richard's release and return from prison in Austria and subsequent war with the King of France. This chronicle does not entail a tournament nor employ the term *tornoi*, however, it does make use of the word *ahatie* (or *ahatine*), an apparent synonym at that time for "tournament" which is found in two romances by Chrétien de Troyes: *La Charrete* and *Cligés*, and in the narrative *Le Maréchal*. The word *ahatie* is germane because it is used not only by Ambroise to describe the battles of the Third Crusade, but also by Chrétien de Troyes and the author of *Le Maréchal* to designate purely chivalric sport.

The last source to note is a bilingual Latin and Old French prose work by Lambert, the Curé d'Ardre. Entitled *Chronique de Guines et d'Ardre*,[23] it was most likely written in the early thirteenth century. It is the ancestral history of Lambert's relatives, starting about the mid-tenth century and continuing through the early thirteenth. This text is helpful in the discussion on what to call the sport.

The Tournament and Its Background

The tournament was a male-dominated competitive sport popular in Europe in the Middle Ages.[24] It likely originated by way of a type of "shock combat" developed by French knights in the late eleventh or early twelfth century.[25] Knights would prepare for war by practicing this new technique, but apparently found it stimulating enough that even when not preparing for combat they would relish in its pursuits. Gradually the exercise gained status as a game or entertainment.[26] Eventually the exercises were consistently undertaken in times of peace, and continued to provide knights an opportunity to hone their military skills in the guise of a game. While the whole theater (soon to be known as the tournament) provided an excellent occasion for athleticism, additionally, it was the ideal situation in which a knight could acquire honor by proving his skill at military combat tempered by courtesy. Knights strove to match, publicly and collectively, their own ability to guide their horse and to maneuver arms against that of their peers. They went to tournaments not only to amuse themselves but also to gain recognition as members of a special group or fraternity.

Perhaps not so surprisingly, despite the sport's obvious popularity among many groups, it was surrounded by controversy. Much of the controversy was generated from the knowledge that tourneying was first banned throughout many lands, including France and England, by the Catholic Church in November 1130 through the Ninth Canon of Decretal issued by the Council of Clermont. This was shortly after the introduction of the sport, if historians' conclusions are correct. The Catholic Church's major concern was that one outcome of the tournament could be an unholy manner of death. The Catholic Church was not alone in its outlawing of tourneying; in the reign of Stephen of England (1135–1154) the event was forbidden. His successor, King Henry II in 1179 also forbade it, but only in England and not in his French territories. In 1209, Philippe II of France had his son Louis sign a document that he would never take part in a tournament.[27] Amazingly, in spite of successive edicts against it, the sport continued to be popular, even though knights were aware of the pronouncement it would bring. In England, perhaps realizing the futile effect of the Papal bans, the holding of a tournament and participation in one gained legal, official status in 1194 when King Richard I issued a decree allowing tourneying to occur in five areas of Great Britain.[28] According to this royal decree, men had to pay a type of registration fee in order to participate. Richard also issued, for a price, licenses to those wishing to sponsor any such event. He well understood that the sport could be profitable and saw its legalization as a way to acquire welcome revenue.[29] Tourneying was still not sanctioned by the Catholic Church, but was at least legal in England to those willing and able to pay the fee. In addition, in permitting tournaments, Richard no doubt hoped to improve the reputation of the English knights and the quality of tournaments through practice. The French were considered the superior tourneyers of the day, and French tournaments were the most highly regarded in the chivalric society, hence it would have been important to the English to ameliorate their abilities.[30]

The identity of the creator of the tournament is unknown, although it is widely believed to have been Geoffrey de Preuilly.[31] What is certain is that the sport is referred to in texts very soon after its believed beginnings, and not solely in edicts against it. There is a *Gesta* in Latin-rhymed verse which mentions the tournament as early as 1137:

> Dum sic agitur apud nos,
> plurali fertur nuntis
> quod Gilius de Cinnio
> mortuus est in tornio.

No matter that the passage tells of a knight's death in a tournament, the text dates from 1138 and clearly uses the word *tornio* to refer to the game rather than a battle.[32] The first attestation of the term, *turnei* (another old spelling of the word) in a purely lyric poem appears in the mid-twelfth century, circa 1146.[33] At this early stage in the development of the term, while it could refer to a tournament as we know it, it still more frequently designated real combat. It was not until the last quarter of the twelfth century that the words *tornoi* and *tornoiement* occur regularly with the more familiar meaning "tournament" has today.[34]

Starting with its birth the tournament continually evolved until it fell out of favor to a large degree in the mid-fifteenth century. It had by then become prohibitively expensive for a knight since by that time he had to furnish his own armor, horse, and arms, all of which cost a great deal, unlike in the early days when a wealthy patron would generally sponsor and provide the *accoûtrements*. The protocol and techniques were constantly changing such that the early, twelfth-century tournaments, where knights used sharp weapons and followed no set rules, bore little resemblance to the mid-fifteenth-century ones that René d'Anjou depicts in his colorful book on the sport; in those, knights used blunted weapons and followed highly-organized guidelines.

Notes

1. Sir Walter Scott, *Ivanhoe*, ed. A.N. Wilson (London: Penguin Books Classics, 1986 reprint).

2. René d'Anjou, *Traité de la forme et devis d'un tournoi*, ed. Edmond Pognon (Paris: Verve, 1946).

3. See for example, Coltman R. Clephan, *The Tournament, Its Periods and Phases* (New York: Frederick Ungar, 1919); Francis Henry Cripps-Day, *The History of the Tournament in England and France* (London: B. Quaritch, 1918); Juliet Barker, *The Tournament in England 1100–1400* (Suffolk: St. Edmundsbury Press, 1986).

4. Paul Meyer, ed., *L'Histoire de Guillaume le Maréchal*, 3 vols (Paris: Reynouard, 1891). Subsequently, this narrative may be referred to as *Le Maréchal*, and the hero by his modern English name, William.

5. Henceforth, Henry the younger may more frequently be called the Young King.

6. "C'est Johan d'Erlée, por veir" (v. 19,189) and "Car Johans s'est bien esprové / qui cest livre a fet e trové" (vv. 19,195–19,196).

7. Since this is not a study on the author of *Le Maréchal*, I will henceforth consider it as an anonymous work.

8. Marie de France, *Les Lais de Marie de France*, ed. Jean Rychner (Paris: Honoré Champion, 1968). All subsequent references, unless otherwise noted, will be to this edition.

9. Gaston Paris, "Les Lais inédits de Tyolet, de Guingamor, de Doon, du Lecheor et de Tydorel," *Romania* 8 no. 1 (1879): 29–72.

10. Paris, "Les Lais inédits," 64–66.

11. Chrétien de Troyes, *Yvain, Le Chevalier au lion*, trans. William W. Kibler (New York and London: Garland Publishing, 1985). Subsequently, this romance may be referred to as *Yvain*.

12. Chrétien de Troyes, *Erec et Enide*, trans. Carleton Carroll (New York and London: Garland Publishing, 1987).

13. Chrétien de Troyes, *Les Romans de Chrétien de Troyes: Le Chevalier de la charrete*, ed. Mario Roques (Paris: Librairie Ancienne Honoré Champion, 1958). Subsequently, this romance will be referred to as *La Charrete*. All subsequent references, unless otherwise noted, will be to this edition.

14. Chrétien de Troyes, *Les Romans de Chrétien de Troyes: Cligés*, ed. Alexandre Micha (Paris: Librairie Ancienne Honoré Champion, 1957).

15. Chrétien de Troyes, *Les Romans de Chrétien de Troyes: Le Conte du Graal*, ed. Felix Lecoy (Paris: Honoré Champion, 1973 and 1975). Subsequently, this romance will be referred to by its more common title, *Perceval*.

16. Hue de Rotelande, *Ipomedon,* ed. A.J. Holden (Paris: Klincksieck, 1979).

17. G.-A. Crapelet, ed., *Partonopeus de Blois* (Paris: L'Imprimerie de Crapelet, 1834).

18. See footnote by editor on page 133.

19. John R. Reinhard, ed*., Amadas et Ydoine* (Paris: Librairie Ancienne Honoré Champion, 1926). All subsequent references, unless otherwise noted, will be to this edition.

20. J-J. Salverda de Grave, ed., *Enéas—Roman du XIIe siècle,* 2 vols (Paris: Honoré Champion, 1964).

21. Guy Raynaud de Lage, ed., *Le Roman de Thèbes*, 2 vols (Paris: Honoré Champion, 1968).

22. Ambroise, *L'Estoire de la guerre sainte: histoire en vers de la troisième croisade,* ed. Gaston Paris (Paris: Imprimerie Nationale, 1897). Subsequently, this chronicle will be referred to as *La Guerre sainte.*

23. Lambert, Curé d'Ardre, *Chronique de Guines et d'Ardre* (Paris: Jules Renouard, 1855.

24. There remains a great deal of controversy about the actual chronological extent of the Middle Ages, as well as when the tournament was practiced. It is widely agreed that the age of tournaments came to an end in 1559 when King Henry II of France was struck in the eye by a lance during a tournament; his injury did not heal and he died shortly after. Juliet Barker's book on the tournament in England covers the time frame of 1100 to 1400. I, myself, tend to believe the sport exists in some form even today, but that is another story and I am not attempting to discuss this belief at this time. Since I will refer to Barker's book throughout, I will use her time frame as a constant for referral to the general age of tournaments, and for lack of a more appropriate term, I will use the "Middle Ages" to refer to the centuries into which I delve.

25. "The tournament seems to have emerged in the late eleventh or early twelfth century at a period when French knights were introducing a new type of shock combat. . . ." Barker, *The Tournament,* 4.

26. Michel Parisse calls it "le divertissement chevaleresque par excellence" in "Le Tournoi en France des origines à la fin du XIIIe siècle" in *Das ritterliche Turnier im Mitterlalter* ed. Josef Fleckenstein (Göttingen: Vandenhœck & Ruprecht, 1985), 175.

27.   Ernest Lavisse, *Histoire de France: Depuis les origines jusqu'à la révolution. Tome troisième: Louis VII–Philippe-Auguste–Louis VIII (1137–1226)*. Ed. by Achille Luchaire (Paris: Librairie Hachette et cie., 1911), 367.

28.   "The holding of tournaments was restricted by Richard to five places or districts, namely between (1) Salisbury and Wilton, (2) Warwick and Kenilworth, (3) Stamford and Warmington, (4) Brackley and Mixbury, and (5) Tickhill and Blyth. To these must be added Smithfield for the use of the citizens of London on Saturdays." Joseph Strutt, *Sports and Pastimes of the People of England* (London: Methusen & Co., 1801), 118. In the *Patent Rolls* of Richard I, August 22, 1194 is the recorded date.

29.   William Stubbs, ed., *Select Charters and Other Illustrations of English Constitutional History*, 8th ed. (Oxford: Clarendon Press, 1895), vol. I; 545.

30.   "In virtually all matters of chivalry and of chivalric culture the French in consequence set the fashion for the English, throughout the whole period from the Norman Conquest down to the Yorkist Age." Juliet Barker and Maurice Keen, "The Medieval English Kings and the Tournament," in *Das ritterliche Turnier im Mittelalter*, ed., Josef Fleckenstein (Göttingen: Vandehœck & Ruprecht, 1985), 212–28; 213.

31.   Barker, *The Tournament*, 5.

32.   The "De Morte Egidii de Cinnio" is in the *Gesta Pontificum Cameracensium: Gestes des Evêques de Cambrai de 1092 à 1138* (Paris: Librairie Renouard, 1880), 204. They are a chronicle of the life seen and experienced in part by the various archbishops of Cambrai. This compilation is not intended as fiction or pure diversion. It purports to recount the events as they occurred. Knowing this, the appearance of the word "tornio" is important for the explicitness of its meaning; on August 12, 1137 Gilles de Chin died in a tournament. It is interesting that in this, a "religious" text, death is mentioned. Such a genre-source is not a detailed part of my literary corpus and warrants a study of its own.

33.   Ulrich Mölk, "Remarques philologiques sur *tornoi(ement)* dans la littérature française des XIIe et XIIIe siècles" in *Badia i Margarit*, Symposium in Honorem Prof. M. de Riquer (Barcelona: Universitat de Barcelona, 1986), 277–87; 277.

34.   ". . . qu'au dernier quart du XIIe siècle, les mots tornoi et tornoiement se rencontrent, avec le sens spécialisé de "tournoi", dans les textes appartenant à n'importe quel genre littéraire. . . ." Mölk, 278. There is clearly an early ambiguity involving the term for the sport of tourneying and a word is necessary concerning *tornoi* (tourney) and *tornoiement* (tournament) (to be used rather interchangeably) as they henceforth will appear. For the most part, no matter the Old French term used, the tournament will designate a peacetime confrontation of two large teams of knights. While most of the sources herein employ the term *tornoi* in reference to such a confrontation, in two works the word *tornoi* does not correspond to the above definition. In these two instances, the word had not yet taken on its specialized meaning and denotes real, as opposed to mock, combat; this will be explored to greater extent later.

Chapter I

Old French Terminology

The rhetoric of the tournament, including the terms used for weapons and for certain techniques, was essentially uniform even in the sport's early stages of development;[1] curiously, the same cannot be said of the actual word to designate the sport itself. Particularly in the early days of tourneying, there was not yet a single fixed word to describe the occasion; to wit, a score of words existed in the Old French[2] language to indicate the game, and Michel Stanesco notes the diversity in the choices:

> Beaucoup de textes n'utilisent pourtant pas ce mot, ou bien l'emploient à concurrence avec toute une série: *ahatine, asemblee, bohort, cembel(s), derei, estor, jouste, mellée, poigneiz, presse, pardon d'armes, trespignées, tupineis, Tables Rondes*; . . .[3]

These particular terms also have varied spellings, by way of illustration: *bohort, bouhourdeïç, bohourt*. Additionally, the word "tournament" was often improperly used in literature.[4]

In the tournament passages, the two terms other than *tournoi* most frequently used to refer to the action are "joust" and "*mêlée*," however, some clarification is crucial at this point. The common view of the tournament, the joust, and the *mêlée* is that all three mean the same thing. In actuality, they do not. The joust was an encounter on horseback between two people. It could occur at any time and anywhere.[5] The word can even be used to describe two men fighting in war, e.g., in *La Charrete* a battle is taking place well before the grand engagement yet the poet uses "joste" to describe a belligerent encounter between two knights: "s'ancontre un chevalier venant / et joste a lui, sel fiert si fort" (vv. 2384–2385). It is clear though that there was a difference in the two meanings of jousting and tourneying and the romance *Ipomedon* also makes such a distinction; before the tournament begins, two friends are talking about the competition which is to take place. During the conversation, one says to the other that they will sleep and eat together, as well as go "al juster e al turneer" (v. 3204). The use of the two separate verbs indicates they were different activities. Jousts did occur during tournaments, but were not restricted to them, thus the joust is a subcategory of the tournament.

A *mêlée* refers to the moment of a much frenetic nature where all the knights were fighting on the field. As such, it describes the chaotic atmosphere that often prevailed at an early tournament, or in real combat for that matter.[6] The *mêlée* was the main form of the tournament because of the large teams that faced each other at the same time. The modern perception of the tournament has been largely influenced by the work of René d'Anjou whose treatise on the sport was a very visual pictorial.[7] In short, the tournament is the grand event where both jousts and *mêlées* undoubtedly occur, but the words are not synonymous.

Without listing every line in which they appear, some examples of the words "joust" and "*mêlée*" in connection with the tournament scenes are as follows: in *Amadas et Ydoine*, "mainte dure joste i ot faite" (v. 4451) and "quant est en l'espesse meslee" (v. 4410); in *Cligés*, the hero defeats anyone who dares joust with him: "que a joste atendre l'osa" (v. 4657). The joust is often conveyed through the verb form as in "Milun" where *juster* appears. As for the word *mêlée*, in "Chaitivel" the spelling *medlee* is used. In the narrative *Le Maréchal*, the terms *joste* and *meslée* (*mellée*) (cf. *Amadas et Ydoine* above) frequently are the spellings of choice. Even some of the rarer terms cited by Stanesco, appear more often in the sources than might be believed. The poem *Amadas et Ydoine* uses the word *bouhourdeïç* to describe the first competition of the narrative. Moreover, the verb *bouhourder* is used in the same text with the present participle *bouhourdant*. Since these spellings occur early in the narrative, one would believe that *bouhourdeïç* was the more common term in the Picard dialect[8] for the sport, and that in the later tournaments described by the poet he would employ the same word. This, however, is not the case; after the initial appearance of the word the author chooses instead to refer to the tournament with a variant of *tournoiement*. In the romance *La Charrete*, among other words, Chrétien de Troyes chooses *ahatine* and *estor*; in his romance *Cligés* he employs *estorz* and *asanblee* as a term for "tournament." In *Erec et Enide*, the word *cenbel* (variation on *cembal*) is used once. Chrétien seems to have been choosing words for poetic effect and perhaps may have been trying to find the one he liked best or he believed most popular. Occasionally, scattered among the different spellings of *tournoi* in *Le Maréchal*, the word *estor* appears. None of the other narratives uses any of these mostly archaic words, but it is evident that there was uncertainty as to what to call the new event. The spellings of the more common term of "tournament" were also many and can be indicated schematically thus:

Histoires

   L'Histoire de Guillaume le Maréchal: torneiement, tornei (nouns)

Lais

   Marie de France: turneiement, turneiz (nouns)

   "Le Lecheor:" tornoier (verb)

   "Doon:" tornoiement (noun), tornoier (verb)

Romans

   Chrétien de Troyes: tornoi, tornoiement (nouns)

   Hue de Rotelande: turneiement, turnei, le turneer (nouns),
         turneer (verb)

   Amadas et Ydoine: tournoiement, tornoi, tornoiement (nouns)

   Partonopeus de Blois: tornoi, tornoiement (nouns), tornoier (verb)

Part of the reason for the many spellings of much the same word lies in the fact that the poets came from different regions, and likely also, different countries, but in good part, the reason is due to the absence of a true set vocabulary for these early days of the sport.

The alternation between *tornei* and *torneiement* or any other orthographical variation was highly due to the instability of the term which applied to this new recreation. Poets were just not certain what name to give it. Furthermore, their choice changed occasionally to suit the rhyme scheme of the narrative, e.g., in *Amadas et Ydoine*, there exists: "si bel et issi cointement / s'enva droit au tournoiement" (vv. 4285–4286); in this example, *tournoiement* rhymes with *cointement*. Further along during the same tournament passage, the poet opted for the shorter form *tornois* to rhyme with *conrois*: "tout arestés est li tornois / quant leur vint sus uns un grant conrois" (vv. 4353–4354). In a more blatant application of this "poetic license," in order to suit his rhyme scheme in *Le Maréchal*, the poet substitutes in the word for an entirely different game which was sometimes, but not always, included at a tournament. The term in question in this passage is a *quinteine*:

par tot furent noveles pleines
que entre Se[i]nt Jame & Valeines
donereit l'en une quinteine.
chescuns a son poeir se peine
de [a]torner isi son afaire
comme a tel bosoigne estuet faire
e por ce fu mis a quinzeine. (vv. 1201–1207)

The prevalent sound in these lines is "eine," stemming from the locale which is Valeines. The poet took care to enhance this ending by composing a number of lines with the very same sound. The *quinteine* was a specific type of contest,[9] but it was not an all-encompassing tournament, yet the poet chose to use *quinteine* in his verse because the rhyme would not have worked with a form of *tornoi*.[10] This tactic is evident because after his clever play with rhymes, he continues the description of the competition, but then refers to it as a *tornei[e]ment* now because, in turn, *quinteine* was no longer convenient to his verse.

While the spelling may differ in the narratives, the meaning and usage of the term *tournoi* is essentially the same in *Le Maréchal*, the *lais* and the romances, and it designates an actual contest between opposing teams. On occasion, though, there is a puzzling use of the term, and at this juncture it is pertinent to note a remark by Ulrich Mölk, who decides, after all, that it did not matter what term was used to describe the tournament in written or spoken French, but that "ce qui était essentiel, par contre, c'était de désigner, par un terme propre, un genre de combat tout à fait caractéristique de la classe chevaleresque."[11] If Mölk is correct in his assessment, and I believe he is, then it will be interesting to see where and why the term *tornoi* is apparently inappropriately used in the texts.

In the classical antiquity narratives the *Roman de Thèbes* and the *Enéas*, the noun *tornoi* does appear, but it does not refer to the same type of event as in *Le Maréchal*, the *lais* and the romances. Mölk observes that "malgré toute stylisation courtoise, il reste le fait que ni le *Roman de Thèbes* ni les autres romans antiquisants antérieurs à 1170 n'emploient les deux mots de *tornoi/tornoiement* dans l'acception de <<tournoi>>."[12] I agree with him in that in both the *Roman de Thèbes* and the *Enéas*, the word *tornoi* is used to describe real combat and not a game of physical prowess. There are in each account, many lines that tell the tale of the battle. The following four representatives substantiate this: "icil tornoi fu merveillex" and "itel gent menee a tornoi" (*Roman de Thèbes*, v. 4631 and v. 4912), and "se rest comanciez li tornoiz" and "vos remanroiz ci al tornoi" (*Enéas*,

v. 7029 and v. 6968). The word *tornoi* is used extensively to designate the battle, not a friendly competition. Although written in twelfth-century French, and incorporating many then-current customs, the two stories nonetheless recount the sieges of Troy and Thebes.[13]

Interestingly, in the *Roman de Thèbes*, there is a distinction between the *tornoi* occurring on the field—siege of Thebes—and a childhood sport of the soldiers they also call a tourney:

> Atant estes vous les enfanz
> dont li plus jeunes ot cent anz.
> Onc ne fu mes par nesun roi
> itel gent menee a tornoi.
> Preuz furent mout en lor jovent,
> a tel jeu jouerent souvent;
> remenbre leur du vasselage
> qu'il orent en leur bon aage. (vv. 4909–4916)

In such a distinction, the author accentuates the duality of the term *tornoi* in his day. The words *a tel jeu* translate as "at such a game," and the verb used is *jouerent* or "played." The particular reference to the noun *tornoi* shows how in childhood these same soldiers now on the battlefield "played" a game which was called the *tornoi*. Yet, at the moment they are discussing their childhood they are engaged in a *tornoi* that is not playful. It is fascinating that the poet interchanges the words; on the one hand, describing the horrific battle with the term *tornoi* yet, on the other, describing an almost idyllic[14] time when the men played a game of the same name. Identifying two separate manifestations with the same term is a result of the infancy of the sport of tourneying and a desire to adapt antiquity to the then-current way of life.

Consider a further remark by Mölk with regard to what he believes a misuse of the term *tornoi*:

> Contrairement aux quatre lais intitulés *Le Fresne, Laustic, Milun* et *Chaitivel* où Marie emploie les trois termes (*turneier, turnei, turneiement*) de la même manière que Chrétien, on hésiterait à attribuer le même sens ("tournoi") à *turneiement*, dans le *Guigemar*. Guigemar, nous dit le texte, se rend, accompagné de nombreux chevaliers, à un turneiement que Meriaduc a proclamé contre son voisin qui est son *ennemi* et avec lequel il est en guerre depuis longtemps. . . . À notre avis, il faudrait traduire le *turneiement* du texte non par "tournoi", mais par "combat" ou "bataille".[15]

According to Mölk, the word *turneiement* is improperly used in "Guigemar." In this case though, I would contend the contrary. Initially, the tournament in the *lai* is a true scheduled contest, one that Merïadus uses as a ruse to lure Guigemar to the castle ("de ci qu'a un turneiement / que Merïadus afia" [vv. 744–745]). Through the verb *afia*, translating closely as "promised to be held,"[16] it is clear that the tournament was indeed announced, although it never took place. In fact, Marie emphasizes that a tournament had been originally scheduled because, as she specifically says, Guigemar leaves the city with all the knights who had gone there "to tourney:" "en la vile n'out chevalier / ki fust alez pur turneier / ke Guigemar n'en meint od sei" (vv. 857–859). What happens the next day, after Guigemar has left the castle, is a *bataille*, indeed, Marie no longer refers to it as a tournament but rather as an assault (she writes the verb form of assault in "al chastel vienent, si l'asaillent" [v. 873]). True, Merïadus was an enemy of his neighbor against whom the tournament was ostensibly directed, yet, unlikely as the politics may appear to the modern reader, it was an ideal trick to get Guigemar in Merïadus' presence. While rather rare and generally frowned upon, tournaments were at times scheduled between feuding factions.[17]

More confusion arises in *Partonopeus de Blois* with the unusual appearance of the verb *tornoier* long before the true tournament takes place: "g'irai as païens tornoier" (v. 2171), but I contend that in this instance, the verb *tornoier* maintains its original meaning of "tourner, faire tourner,"[18] and is not inappropriately used as a synonym for war, much less refers to any competition. Partonopeus is planning to take his two thousand men into combat; they will turn and constantly move. The noun *tornoi* is never used in this particular passage, and therefore, there is no suggested association with a tournament (which might lead to a misinterpretation of the verb *tornoier* in this line). Still yet, a more confusing situation, arises in the narrative *Le Maréchal*. Therein is a seemingly out of place usage of the noun *torneis*. The poet at one point is describing a siege which he first refers to as a battle ("quer trop fu cruelz la bataille" [v. 1001]), but later refers to this same siege as having been a *torneis* ("la fu li torneis maintenu" [v. 1010]). As Mölk would contend, it is an improper use of the word *torneis* because the circumstances indicate a siege. Curiously, the editor of this particular chronicle, Paul Meyer, has an opposing opinion on the very event and identifies it as a tournament.[19] Meyer comes to his decision because of an early portion of the scene in which ladies and heralds are present (vv. 967–979). Such personalities were not generally in attendance at a battle, hence Meyer's conclusion.

Despite these apparent misuses, the tendency to use a form of *tornoi* to depict war is more understandable when one considers that in the poems, authors frequently use the verb for "combat" (*cumbat*) in describing a tournament. Thus are described two knights participating in *Ipomedon's* tournament: "e se cumbatent vassaument / Capaneüs se cumbat ben" (vv. 4874–4875). Later, the author compares the tournament field which is strewn with bodies, to a battlefield: "or sunt desuz, or sunt desus / cum de guerre est custume e us" (vv. 6145–6146). Decidedly, there were numerous similarities between the tournament and wartime combat; for all practical purposes, a medieval tournament is a mock battle, it just happens to occur in peacetime.[20] In addition, most of the *accoûtrements* in a tournament are identical to those of war. For example, here is a typical description of the *tornoi* in the *Enéas*, which, embellished as it may be, refers to real combat:

Bien fiert de lance et mialz d'espee,
a grant mervoille fu dotee;
ne giete pas son cop an vain;
qui feruz estoit de sa main,
ne languissoit pas longuement,
mire ne valoit noiant,
la mort suoit son cop toz tens;
n'i avoit noiant de deffens
por bon halberc, por fort escu. (vv. 7039–7047)

To continue the comparison, here is a passage from *Ipomedon* where the *tornoi* is truly the peacetime competition:

e meinte lance i ad frossee
e meinte cele i ad voidee,
meinte sambue dessiree,
de vermeil sanc envolupée,
meint bon escu tut estroé,
pleié meint heaume e enfundé
et meint bon hauberk demaillé. (vv. 4831–4837)

Lastly, the following is a passage from the historical chronicle *La Guerre sainte* describing the men as they leave ready and equipped for crusading, i. e., fighting:

tantes beles riches banieres
e penuncels de granz manieres.
tanz veissiez la filz de meres,

tanz lignages, nevuz e freres,
tant bons haubercs, tant bons parpoinz,
tanz armees genz si qu'as poinz,
tantes lances e tantes glaives,
tant ne vit l'em el tens noz aives,
tantes cleres espees cheres,
tanz biaus serjanz od bones cheres! (vv. 9769–9778)

It is quite evident that the armaments are the same—*espees, lances, halberc, escu*. The reason for these similarities is the common military origin of the two phenomenons. Such equipment and armaments had existed for some time; the game had not. Poets simply took words from the vocabulary of warfare already familiar to their audience and applied them to the sport of tourneying. Additionally, a good portion of the vocabulary came from the everyday language, hence, the term for men is *chevalers* in *Ipomedon* and *chevaliers* in the *Enéas* and *La Guerre sainte*.

In reference to Marie de France and a particular *lai* she wrote, Elizabeth Poe remarks:

> The catalogue of participants according to homeland (vv. 77–79) and her remark about their eagerness to come to the tournament resemble so closely certain passages in *Guillaume le Maréchal* that one has to wonder whether there already existed in the 1170's a rhetoric of the tournament. . . .[21]

Certainly, Poe brings up a good point and I would concur that there was a certain "rhetoric of the tournament" probably as early as the 1170's; thus not surprisingly, a whole vocabulary evolved just as the sport did. Its evolution in the *romans* is observed by Michel Parisse:

> Le tournoi du XIIe siècle est différent de celui du XIIIe siècle et les romans donnent l'image de leur évolution. Le vocabulaire évolue et cela se remarque dans la langue des romanciers. Des nouveautés sont créées, une nouvelle législation s'impose, l'espace politique se modifie; tout cela passe dans la littérature.[22]

Granted, Parisse specifies *romans*, yet the same should hold true for any genre. Much of the rhetoric or vocabulary of the sport was available early on because it existed essentially as part of the military world; it did not have to be created. And this same rhetoric later endured changes as pointed out by Parisse.

Stylistically speaking, the literary accounts of warfare and tournaments were also alike. In order to emphasize the importance or fierceness of either event, the poets often repeated adverbs or other words. In the preceding examples, *meint* is repeated in *Ipomedon* and *tant* is so repeated in *La Guerre sainte*. In this next passage, taken from *Partonopeus de Blois*, the poet emphasizes *moult*:

Moult set et de lance et d'escu,
moult joste sovent et menu,
moult est esgardés de la tor,
moult le proisent li jugéor.
Tant a cevaliers abatus,
moult en est doutés et cremus. (vv. 8039–8044)

No matter then the content of the narrative, the poets still adhered to a particular literary style, a tendency which lends partially to the confusion for understanding the sport.

Another term—referring to the tournament as well—deserves some examination. The word *ahatine* is defined by Frédérick Godefroy as "forme variée de *aatine, ahatine*, pris dans le sens de vif ardeur."[23] In *La Guerre sainte*, the word *aatie* is used three times to describe vigorous attacks ("la veissiez granz aaties" [v. 3875], also see v. 6587 and v. 11,344). The editor of *Le Maréchal*, where it appears likewise, translates *par aatie* as *par défi* or *à l'envi*[24] (see line 6055 "que par a[a]tie a tut pris"). Curiously, a variation of the word is found in *Cligés*: "car cui il fiert par anhatie" (v. 4750). The modern translator of this romance also renders *par anhatie* as "challenge," the English meaning. In *La Charrete*, a later romance in the sequence of Chrétien's works, the word appears five times with variants and takes on a more focused meaning than it had in *Cligés*. In at least three of the five occurrences, there is no doubt that the word refers to the tournament and is, in fact, translated by the editor as such: "si s'an vindrent a l'anhatine" (v. 5765), "l'anhatine ensi departi" (v. 6055), and "a l'ahatine de Noauz" (v. 6069). This last example is part of a sentence which uses a form of the verb *tornoier* ("la ou en avoit tornoié [v. 6068]). The use of the verb *tornoié* in conjunction with the noun *ahatine* supports the view that the words are synonymous.

One has to wonder why *tornoi* became the definitive term as opposed to *anhatine*. Marie-Luce Chênerie would like to attribute Chrétien's choice of *ahatine* to its connotations of challenge: ". . .Le mot *ahatine* que Chrétien de Troyes emploie pour ces tournois, a des connotations de *furor*, de défi, de concurrence."[25] She is aware that "l'origine du mot est incertaine,"[26] but believes the word is based on the Germanic root *at* for *souffle*.[27] Chênerie, then, would associate *ahatine* with a fierce attack, which must have indeed characterized many tournaments. Parisse attributes the selection of *tornoiement* over *ahatine* to the lance that was employed in the game. He observes that when adversaries "turned around" (origins of *tourner*) each other with a sword, the maneuver was not referred to as a tournament.[28] When however, the lance was used as a weapon, if a knight missed striking an opponent with it, he could do a turnabout and attack again, hence the word *tournoiement*:

> "Le tournoiement" est bien une façon de dénommer le jeu à la lance ou *hastiludium*; . . . Ce que Geoffroi aurait découvert, c'est un nouveau jeu de cavaliers, un combat. . . . Pourtant c'est bien le mot tournoiement qui a été choisi pour le désigner; cela signifie que dans cet exercice militaire la place de la lance est devenue importante.[29]

In King Richard I's edict to legalize the sport of tourneying, the chronicler William of Newburgh, acknowledges that the sport was called "tournament" in the language of the people, the vulgar tongue: "quæ torneiamenta vulgo dicuntur."[30] Newburgh's remark suggests that the choice of the word *tornoi*, as opposed to any other word such as *ahatine*, was due primarily to its common usage among the people. It could be recognized by the aristocracy, as well as by the peasantry. Perhaps *ahatine* like *quinteine* was too precise a term, and *tornoi* being more general and common as Newburgh observes, won out. Whatever the true reasons for favoring *tornoi*, there was obviously some attempt to popularize *ahatine* because it does appear in early works as a synonym for tournament.

The similarities in the tournament descriptions of *Le Maréchal*, the fictional works, and the *romans d'antiquité* allow certain conclusions to be drawn about the rhetoric of the sport. The rhetoric of the techniques and weapons existed no doubt because of militaristic origins. The rhetoric to describe the opening, middle, and closure of the competition was due mainly to the borrowings of everyday life. The term for the game however, was clearly variable. The two *romans d'antiquité* may be regarded as precursors of the gradual shift in meaning of the term *tornoi* for in describing real battles, they use the word that was soon to be restricted to the developing sport. The other sources reveal the variations of the term and the attempts to establish *tornoi* as a popular word.

While in the early years the vocabulary in question was part of everyday language both written and spoken (that is terms for location, setting, maneuvers, and arms), for many years there continued to be much confusion over what to call the actual sport itself. Most noticeably, as the works exhibit and Michel Stanesco has sorted out, the precise term naming the sport of tourneying was initially difficult to choose. Each author, just as Mölk says, was ultimately trying to find an ideal word to designate a type of combat unique to knights. Suffice it to say, the tournament was extremely well-known, and its popularity and newness led to various authors wishing to interchange the term "tournament" with that of true battle.

Notes

1. See chapter on weapons and techniques.

2. There were numerous terms in Latin as well to describe the tournament, but to cite one example, Lambert d'Ardre writes "vel in militando" (339) at one point in his chronicle, which he translates on the opposite page into Old French as "joustes et tournois" (338).

3. Michel Stanesco, *Jeux d'errance du chevalier médiéval* (Leiden: E.J. Brill, 1988), 74.

4. Interestingly, instead of the term "*tournament*" Juliet Barker prefers to use the term "hastiludes (to give them the widest generic term) . . ." *The Tournament*, 1. Additionally, in order to alleviate exhausting the use of the word "tournament", various terms such as "competition, event, engagement" among others, will be used on occasion. This in no way implies anything but a rather synonymous word for the sport.

5. As Parisse notes: "Avec le tournoi paraît la joute, qui est l'affrontement isolé de deux individus. Le mot vient du latin *juxta* ou *juxtare*, qui contient la notion d'ajout et de réunion." Parisse, 184.

6. Michel Pastoureau points out: "Le tournoi du XIIe siècle n'oppose pas deux individus mais deux troupes d'hommes d'armes, certains à cheval, d'autres à pied, et la belle ordonnance qui précède l'engagement se transforme rapidement en une mêlée tumultueuse, où, comme sur les champs de bataille, l'on combat par petits groupes, en faisant usage de signes de reconnaissance." Michel Pastoureau, *La Vie quotidienne en France et en Angleterre au temps des chevaliers de la table ronde (XIIe–XIIIe siècles)* (Paris: Hachette, 1976), 133–34.

7. In reference to the types of images as René provides, Noël Denholm-Young says "we must dismiss such pictures from our mind in thinking of the tournament from A.D. 1150 to 1350. It is for the most part not a matter of individual jousting, but a mass-meeting of side against side, resulting in a mêlée which differed little from real war." Noël Denholm-Young, "The Tournament in the Thirteenth Century," in *Studies in Medieval History Presented to Frederick Maurice Powicke*, ed. R.W. Hunt, W. A. Pantin and R.W. Southern (Oxford: The Clarendon Press, 1948), 240–68; 240.

8. Picard being the language of the work.

9. The *quinteine*: "There were many variants of the game, but essentially it consisted of an object, usually a shield, fixed to the top of a pole at which the horseman aimed his lance; it could also be used by men on foot attacking a mannikin on top of a pole with swords and clubs." Barker, *The Tournament*, 150.

10. My observation is corroborated by Paul Meyer, editor of *Le Maréchal*. See his note in the glossary definition of *quinteine*.

11. Mölk, 286.

12. Mölk, 280.

13. "Les traits nouveaux que nous observons dans le *Roman de Thèbes*, persistent et s'affirment dans celui d'*Enéas* où, vers 1160, un poète normand prétendit travestir à la mode du XIIe siècle la riche matière de l'*Enéide*." Robert Bossuat, *Le Moyen Age* (Paris: J. De Gigord, 1931), 87.

14. I choose to say idyllic because the characters in this scene are extremely aged men, the youngest is over one hundred. Their age momentarily eliminates the seriousness of the battle and begins a more serene atmosphere which continues for the next six lines before reality is once again evident.

15. Mölk, 283.

16. The editor Jean Rychner translates the verb *afia* into Modern French as from *promettre de le tenir*, hence the English translation above. See Rychner, 293.

17. See chapter on literary device. As Denholm-Young says, "they could be, and especially in the first half of the thirteenth century they were, a focus for baronial discontent." Denholm-Young, 241. To be sure, Denholm-Young refers to the early thirteenth-century tournament, whereas "Guigemar" dates from approximately 1170, but since the tournament had not yet begun to change radically by the early thirteenth century, Denholm-Young's statement should apply to the "Guigemar" *lai*.

18. Frédéric Godefroy, *Dictionnaire de l'Ancienne Langue française et de tous ses dialectes du IXe au XVe siècle* (Paris: F. Vieweg, 1885).

19. As he says, "on voit que nous sommes en pleine fantaisie. Le poète raconte un tournoi et non une action de guerre." Meyer, *Le Maréchal*, vol. III, p. 18 (footnote 4).

20. In J.J. Jusserand's words, the two events are basically synonymous: "Les jeux ressemblaient à la guerre et la guerre ressemblait aux jeux." J.J. Jusserand, "Les Sports dans l'ancienne France," *Revue de Paris*, no. 10 (Mai, 1900): 288–327; 293.

21. Elizabeth W. Poe, "The Problem of the Tournament in *Chaitivel*," in *In Quest of Marie de France, a Twelfth-Century Poet*, ed. Chantal A. Maréchal (Lewiston, New York: Edwin Mellen Press, 1992), 175–192; 181.

22. Parisse, 203.

23. Godefroy, vol. 1.

24. Meyer, *Le Maréchal*, vol. III, 334.

25.   Marie-Luce Chênerie, *Le Chevalier errant dans les romans arthuriens en vers des XIIe et XIIIe siècles* (Geneva: Droz, 1986), 439.

26.   Chênerie, *Le Chevalier,* 439 (footnote 103).

27.   Ibid.

28.   Parisse, 182.

29.   Ibid.

30.   Richard Howlett, ed., *Historia Rerum Anglicarum*, part 2, vol. 82 of *Rerum Brittannicarum Medii Ævi Scriptores*, 102 vols (London: Longman & Co., 1885), 422.

Chapter II

Tournament Preparations

There are two kinds of preparation of the literary tournament. One is how the author prepared the reader for the tournament about to be presented; the other involves what the character-knight had to do in order to ready himself for the event. As a literary device, preparing the reader for the tournament includes, among other things, providing: discourses on individual chivalric qualities, selections and/or identification of participants, rivalries between nationalities or teams, or possibly the author's personal opinions. In preparation for the tournament, the character-knight, most importantly, had to procure equipment, and at times, had other things to prepare.

In *Partonopeus de Blois*, the first indications of the tournament begin in line 6547, but it is not until line 7925 that the competition actually starts. Thus, it takes the author 1378 verses to progress from the announcement to the tournament itself. Throughout these 1378 lines, he provides certain practical information, such as the location and who will attend. The author also takes the time to give: his own personal opinions on several subjects, particular conversations between characters, and, most importantly, accounts of the hardships the hero must overcome to arrive finally at the event. The lengthy literary preparation gives the author the chance to express what emotional fluctuations the main characters experience (due to various dilemmas) in getting to the tournament. Such a tactic is for the benefit of the reader, who can now share in the experiences and appreciate the hero's eventual participation in the competition almost as much as he does.

In *Ipomedon*, the tournament is discussed and decided upon by *la Fiere* on line 2492, but the day of the event does not arrive until line 3602 when suddenly the young maiden awakes to the noise of the action: "E leve la noise e le brut." The literary preparation in this romance involves 1110 lines which serve to tell what happens during the four-month wait before the event. The long introduction is important in setting up the situation of the hero Ipomedon before the combat, so the reader knows exactly what Ipomedon is scheming. When the day arrives for the start, the reader hopes the hero is as successful in tourneying as he has been in creating illusions about his talents.

There is very little build-up for the two detailed tournaments (of interest to the plot), in *Amadas et Ydoine*. The arrival of the day of the first tournament in fact, is merely alluded to and has no build-up ("Ensi avint qu'a un haut jour" [v. 838]). The day's competition is over approximately sixty lines later. In this first tournament, Amadas does not compete, and since they do not help elevate his status, no details of the action are given. When the second tournament in question appears, in which Amadas does compete, the author takes noticeably more time to introduce the event and describe the combat that later ensues. Amadas learns of this upcoming tournament in line 4081; it does not begin until line 4249, or rather 168 lines later. These 168 lines are informative and practical because they tell how Amadas comes to his decision to compete, then they speak of his journey to the location. At this point, there is no need to recreate an emotional, expressive scene because Amadas no longer has seemingly unsurmountable obstacles to overcome in order to compete nor does he experience emotional highs and lows that are of interest to the tournament.

Undoubtedly because of the brevity of the *lais*, Marie de France writes only short literary preparations for the tournaments, but they do prove to be interesting. In "Guigemar" the build-up entails thirteen lines that tell: who decides to sponsor the tournament, who invites Guigemar and why he is invited, and how many companions arrive with the hero. These are essential points for the understanding of the event's manifestation, even though it does not actually take place. In the *lai* "Milun," Marie gives no advance notice of the tournament, and merely says that the knights gather at the locale; twelve lines later, the tournament begins. What is significant in these twelve lines is that Marie manages to: mention the nationalities of the teams, point out Milun's good qualities, and allow her hero to find his adversary. The pattern is basically the same for "Chaitivel" where in a short span of thirty-seven lines, a brief list of the teams, a reference to preliminary customs, and the spot from where the sponsor is watching, are presented. In Marie's *lais* there is a concentration of many of the same details that are developed at greater length in the romances. She is aware of the shortness expected of the genre, and needs to decide what information is most pertinent to the scene at hand. Obviously, who participates, where the tournament is held, and what the hero is like are certain important factors which necessitate inclusion in the compact framework of the *lais*.

Whereas Marie de France limits the build-up to a tournament, the same truly cannot be said of Chrétien de Troyes. In *Erec et Enide*, the preparation for the tournament includes mentioning that Gawain pledges himself to one team, and that Melis and Meliadoc pledge themselves to another. In all, eight lines are used to get to the day of the tournament where in line 2098, "li tornoiz assanble et ajoste." Subsequently, it takes Chrétien another twenty-two lines to get to the actual meeting of the teams ("tuit s'antre vienent a eslais" [v. 2120]). Chrétien is quite intent on creating an impressive visual effect and with these twenty-two preparatory lines he describes the many colors of equipment, and many tokens of love. He purposely prolongs the action for aesthetic reasons, and since he has no real constraints on length, there is no need for him merely to hint at anything when in-depth, it might be more valuable to the scene. This is no doubt the case when he spends forty-two lines preparing for the tournament in *Cligés*. He uses these lines to create more dimension to the event by "eavesdropping" on some conversations between knights concerning their peers. What is "heard" from the conversations is talk of who is participating and their personalities—insights which help understand the on-goings out on the field. As soon as the knights have finished their discussion, the tournament begins ("Maintenant li estors comance" [v. 4642]).

Chrétien, as ever, not hindered by stylistic expectations, spends 229 lines in preparation of the tournament in *La Charrete*. He spends significantly more time here because this tournament is less typical than most, and he needs to emphasize some of the peculiarities since they are thematically important. Some of the peculiarities elucidated are who organized the event and why they did, and the predicament of one particular participant. Chrétien also needs to convey the importance of this competition. He, in part, does it justice by confirming that the Queen of the land will be in attendance. After such anticipation, the day arrives and the combat begins ("Que il ancomancent l'estor" [v. 5596]). Decidedly, the tournament turns out to be as peculiar, important, and exciting as the build-up had suggested.

In the last tournament in Chrétien's romances, found in *Perceval*, Gawain finds out about the contest when he encounters a squire who tells him about it ("Sire, a un tornoiement va" [v. 4805]). It then takes

Chrétien 182 lines to explain why it is taking place, and to describe the personalities of certain characters. What is interesting about this series of lines is that the reader must "wait" for the tournament by reading the 182 lines, however, the characters themselves do not, rather they begin the contest once Gawain arrives in the town. Clearly, Chrétien revels in the literary preparation of a tournament in order to foster a certain kinship or spirit of the event. In reading all it takes to get to a tournament, the reader can begin to experience the mood and in turn share in the adventure. Chrétien obviously keeps his audience in mind as he writes.

Since there are so many tournaments in the biographical narrative *Le Maréchal*, the discussion of their literary preparations will be limited to several, but certainly not all. In Tournament 1, the tournament is mentioned in line 1203 but does not begin until line 1303. In these one hundred lines, the author gives the locale and the nationalities of parties geared to compete; he also describes a small dilemma experienced by his hero, and shows how his hero overcomes this dilemma. In Tournament 2, the first indication of the contest is in line 1383 and the supposed beginning of it in line 1411. The beginning is a bit hard to determine since all the poet writes is that the knights arm themselves ("La ou li chival[i]er s'armoient"). The twenty-eight lines it takes the author to prepare for the tournament seem relatively few and the action rushed, but justifiably so because they parallel and thus succeed in conveying the haste William makes to get to this tournament. He finds out about it quite late, and when he is in a different region, but since he wants sorely to go, he receives permission to leave and rides quickly, day and night: "Tant cheva[l]che & jor & nuit" (v. 1408). He arrives with just enough time to get off his horse and get armed ("Il desendi hastivement, / Armer se fist molt vistement" [vv. 1413–1414]). Through the brief build-up, the author manages to convey the sense of urgency and desire felt by William.

Elsewhere in the narrative, for Tournament 6, the author increases the build-up to sixty-four lines in which he shows how William takes leave of his lord, talks about the great men who are going to participate, and gives names and nationalities of certain more illustrious competitors. Once again, William is in another region, a detail which forces him, and a companion, to journey to the site of the competition. They have an adequate amount of time, but still have to make haste and not dally ("De lor esrer molt se hastérent; / Tant espleitiérent, tant esrérent / Que il parvindrent a cel li[e]u" [vv. 2897–2899]). There is a sense of urgency in the verb used (*hastèrent*) and the adverb (*tant*), but this urgency, at least for the reader, is soon eliminated because then there are forty lines describing those knights already in-situ just milling about; eventually William arrives and the tournament begins. As is often the case, for the next event (Tournament 8), William must journey quickly to the competition. The day of the tournament has apparently already arrived when William appears because the knights are already gathering. Yet, even though the hero has arrived on the very day, the contest is not actually described for another eighty-two lines, and for good reason. The passage immediately preceding the true start of the contest consists of a short story involving William, some ladies, and a herald. Such a build-up to the eventual tournament is used to character-profile the hero, showing how generous and talented he is.

In Tournament 12, the preparation for the contest is much longer than previously seen, and consists of 338 lines (vv. 4458–4796). Instead of a line or two saying the tournament is impressive, the author achieves a greater effect by specifically naming a large number of knights; he takes the time to enumerate them by name or title, and give qualities to accompany them. By the time the list is completed, the anticipation is such that the reader, along with the knights, should be brimming with haste for the tournament to start. Finally, when it does begin, the author diverges for a quick auditory reflection in pointing out that due to the great numbers of participants, there is consequently a great deal of noise ("Ainz [i out] grant noise e grant bruit" [v. 4799]). This particular tournament is well supplied with information whereas the next one, Tournament 13, is not. It is first mentioned on line 4977, but including the action of the competition, ends sixty-eight lines later. This passage also contains a short introduction of eleven lines which says who will be in attendance, and gives an assurance that the author is telling the truth (in case anyone should doubt the account). And, the narrative build-up to the last tournament under discussion, Tournament 14, consists of a short twenty-seven lines pertinent to the tournament inasmuch as they explain why William actually attends. He did not intend to compete, but does so after conceding to the Young King's wishes. As often seen in *Le Maréchal*, the literary preparation for this tournament is used to character-profile William since it recognizes how loyal he is to the Young King.

Truly, William Marshal is the primary subject of the biographical narrative, but on occasion in the verses leading to a tournament, the author lauds other people or makes personal comments as well. For example, at Tournament 11, he praises the Young King Henry and the practice of chivalry.[1] The poet emphasizes the Young King's role in the survival of chivalry, inherent in which is the sport of tourneying. Also inherent is the author's favorable opinion of the sport which forms the nucleus of *chevalerie*. Such personal comments by a poet are not uncommon, however, in the *histoire* of William Marshal, the tournament build-ups are most frequently used to focus on the central figure of the work rather than used as convenient sounding boards.

While it is not openly apparent, in comparing the build-ups to the tournaments in the various works, one realizes that there are several determining factors. One of which is if success in a given tournament is crucial to the hero's reputation, the author will provide a detailed build-up. In addition to previous examples, consider the first tournament alluded to in *Amadas et Ydoine*. The tournament has little to do with the hero, in turn, not much is said beforehand to portray the event as a magnificent occasion. Elsewhere, in *Yvain*, tournaments are merely alluded to or noted in passing as when Yvain and Gawain have just returned from a tournament ("Et furent la voille devant / revenu del tornoiemant" [vv. 2685–2686]). Gawain fought well there, but because a long build-up or detailed account of the tournament would have served little purpose to further enhancing the hero's reputation, Chrétien devotes only four lines to mentioning it even occurred. The importance of a tournament, then, more often than not, is implicitly indicated in the literary preparation to it, whether through the information the author divulges or the length it receives. This is a consistent pattern in the works, the significance of which is its relation to the hero's reputation.

Quite a deal of time has been spent on how the authors prepare the readers for the tournament in, perhaps, creating a great sense of anticipation with many lines, or on the contrary, rushing into the action and using a few lines. Now it is time to see how the knights themselves prepare for the event. The first example of any knightly preparation is taken from *Cligés*. Cligés begins his journey from Constantinople to Britain with just one set of armor and four horses. Upon his arrival in Britain, he learns of a four-day tournament, and if he is to carry out successfully the plan he expects to execute, he then must procure three more sets of armor. He sends his squires off to get the equipment ("Si lor comande a aporter / Trois peires d'armes desparoilles" (vv. 4554–4555). They seem to have no trouble doing so ("A Londres vienent et si truevent / Apareillié quanque il quierent" [vv. 4564–4565]), and return quickly with their acquisitions. Decidedly, a knight could obtain the necessary equipment relatively easily, although probably not a preferred practice since he would be unfamiliar with the equipment. Yet, this task is the only explicit preparation Cligés is shown to need before the tournament and he now awaits the day.

The obvious necessity of procuring equipment was part of a knight's preparation, one could hardly compete without it, and there were various means of actually getting one's self equipped. Those knights who do not travel with their own supplies could purchase them as just mentioned when presumably Cligés does by sending his squires off to London; others borrow supplies, as is the case for Lancelot and Partonopeus de Blois. Some knights are furnished equipment by friends, patrons, or others. Urrake (Mélior's sister), procures and gives equipment to Partonopeus de Blois so he can compete in the romance of the same name. He is later stripped of this first set of equipment, but again is lent some more. Amadas in his tale is without any equipment when he wishes to compete at Lucca, yet is graciously and generously outfitted by his host:

> S'est ricement apparilliés
> Car li ostes, comme cortois,
> Li a trouvé rice harnois
> Vallet, esquiier et serjant. (*Amadas et Ydoine*, vv. 4232–4235)

Consequently, Amadas is able to go to the tournament extremely well-dressed ("Mult ricement aparilliés" [v. 4255]). In a passage in *Le Maréchal*, the Young King is willing to compete in a tournament, provided he will be furnished with the proper equipment ("E dist, se tant faire peüst / Que chivals e armes eüst, / Qu'il alast molt voluntiers" [vv. 2477–2479). The sport was not elite to such a degree that borrowed equipment was frowned upon; any armor of good quality would suffice.

In his very first tournament, William Marshal is a veritable newcomer, and certainly not wealthy. He has no horse nor can he dress well ("Sire, ge n'ai point de chival / Si'n sui trop mal aparilliez" [*Le Maréchal*, vv. 1224–1225]). He has to rely on the generosity of his lord chamberlain in order to compete. Of course, with his natural ability, he is subsequently able to take prisoners and what they own, even their horses. William eventually establishes himself as a good knight and accumulates riches, and after such time, unlike his very first endeavor, his only real preparation for tournaments is to get to the locale and get dressed, procedures which are not always terribly simple.

These are all significant passages because they indirectly note the expenses needed to be able to compete. It has already been mentioned that the later tournament was a costly affair, and part of the demise of the sport was that the knights themselves had to furnish their own *accoûtrements*. Since it had become terribly expensive, few could afford such luxuries and the sport went into a rapid decline. Noticeably, in the early days, knights were furnished with the necessities by wealthy sponsors or they could acquire their trappings by performing well and capturing their prisoners' belongings. These methods of being equipped allowed knights to concentrate on the techniques of the sport without too much thought to the expenses.

Besides the actual procurement of equipment, there are other things to be done before the tournament; some are more practical in nature. At some point, weapons and armor must be polished or cleaned to keep them in good shape. One of the best and longest descriptions of this task is found in *Le Maréchal*, in preparation for the first tournament:

Tote nuit funt cil chivalier
Haubers roller, chauces freier
& atorner lor armeüres
& colier[e]s & covertures,
Seles & freins, peitrals & cengles,
& fors estriés & contrecengles.
Li autre lur hieaumes assai[e]nt,
Qu'al bosoign aesiez les aient. . .
Lors veïsiez destre & senestre
Enarmer coiphes & ventailles,
& meitre las parmi les mailles.
Molt se peinent de l'ace[s]mer
Al meuz ke il sevent araier.
Tote la nuit se traval[i]érent,
Poi dormirent & molt veilli[é]rent. (vv. 1231–1250)

This passage is quite long yet significant because it shows how much excitement is generated by a tournament. The *chevaliers* have rubbed, cleaned, tried on, looked at, and turned over their helmets, shoes, saddles, and the rest of their equipment. No doubt, there was a certain importance to cleaning, shining and admiring one's equipment before a tournament, but such acts are essentially absent in any other early accounts of tournaments so this is a rare example of such minute details.

Another more practical preparation takes place on the day of the event, when knights must lace up their helmets and get on their horses: "Tantost laciérent lor ventailles / e lor heames e si montérent" (*Le Maréchal*, vv. 3522–3523). When the men arrive on the field for action in *Erec et Enide*, they too, lace their helmets ("Iluec vit an le jor lacier / maint hiaume, de fer et d'acier [vv. 2109–2110]). In the romance *Perceval*, squires run to prepare saddles and horses ("As armes corent escuier / et as chevax, et mestent seles" [vv. 4924–4925]). The second day of this tournament, knights do not ride fully dressed to the field but rather, put on their armor at the edges of the field. Thus, it was more convenient to dress elsewhere, but not a prerequisite. In *Ipomedon*, there are few preparations noted for the tournament itself except the arrival of the hero and the putting on of his armor.

A more traditional preparation or procedure is the placement outside one's door of the shield. This is to locate easily where each participant is staying, and also render importance to the event through the knowledge of just whom is participating. It was necessary though, to be familiar with the heraldry on the shields or seeing the shield would be of little value. This procedure appears each night prior to the following day's action in *Cligés*; for example: "Et fet a l'uis levers la voie / les armes verz metre an presant" (vv. 4668–4669), and "Et fet isnelement fors treire / l'escu vermoil et l'autre ator" (vv. 4760–4761).

In a rare acknowledgment of religious practices, in *Partonopeus de Blois*, the morning of the tournament, Partonopeus and his friend, Gaudins, hear mass: "Messe ont oïe et sont armé" (v. 7865). This reference is of particular interest because one's attendance at mass is a detail not often found in conjunction with the tournament, it certainly does not appear as a frequent preparation. Most religious notions are vague or omitted in the literary tournament accounts, undoubtedly, as mentioned before, due to the Catholic Church's feelings towards the spectacle. Line 7865 is of additional interest and significance because it pairs, in the same sentence, religious and purely secular elements: the two knights heard mass, but also armed themselves.

The early tournament pitted two teams against each other, it was not solely an individual endeavor; consequently, it was necessary to choose a team. Decidedly, the extent of the knightly preparations in

Erec et Enide concerns such a practice where knights pledge (*fiança*) themselves to one side ("Mes sire Gauvains s'avança / qui d'une part le fiança" [vv. 2091–2092]). This example is interesting because it shows that the early tournament was in many respects, spontaneous; the choice of which team to represent could be made the day of the competition. Certainly, it was not a fixed and obligatory rule to know ahead of time one's affiliation. In *La Charrete*, Lancelot also chooses a team, but it is not the most important thing he does; it happens to be the fourth important thing he does to ready himself for the contest. The first thing he does is obtain freedom to compete, since he is being held captive; secondly, he must procure the necessary equipment, which he does; thirdly, he must travel to the locale.

Even though it may appear that Lancelot's asking permission to leave and compete is unusual and only done because he is a prisoner, it is not a unique example. Oftentimes, knights who were not being held captive had to ask for permission to join in a tournament. This is understandable because most of them were in the employ of someone or they had certain obligations, therefore, they frequently had to ask for temporary leave to participate in a tournament. Cligés has to ask his uncle and his beloved Fenice to travel to King Arthur's realm. Ipomedon takes leave of his father and friends ("Ipomedon ad cungé pris / De sun pere e de ses amis" [*Ipomedon*, vv. 2637–2638]). Even William must take leave of his lord on a few occasions: "Congié e[n] kuist a son seignor" (*Le Maréchal*, v. 1394), and "Congié en quist a son seignor" (*Le Maréchal*, v. 2886). Once permission is obtained, they revel in the sport.

All said, the literary preparations for the tournament varied from author to author, and from knightly character to knightly character. There were some common traits that have been elucidated but since each tournament was different, there exists a variety of preparations as well.

Note

1.   See chapter on literary device for the original verse.

Chapter III

The Announcement and The Wait

The announcement of the tournament and the wait before its commencement proved to be extremely important elements for the success of a tournament. In conjunction with these is also the time of year it was to be held. The announcement needed to be widespread to entice many illustrious knights to compete. The duration of wait after the declaration of the event had to be, on the one hand, long enough to allow ample travelling time to a tournament locale and, on the other, short enough to keep the impetuous knight from losing interest. The preference was for relatively dry weather so armor would not rust and not be too brutally hot; naturally the ideal season was spring for its moderate weather and because in part, it tended to create a rejuvenated atmosphere after the cold winter months, thus adding a psychological element to the sport. These factors, which help separate the tournament from other medieval sports, appear in fictitious and historical accounts, and sometimes are very important in the former as the following will explicate.

The tournament in later years was announced in a much more formal manner from the era of these works; in fact, much in the manner that René d'Anjou describes in his illustrated book. Michel Pastoureau also notes that "le seigneur . . . doit . . . en faire crier les jours et le lieu dans toute la région alentour. Il doit en outre envoyer des messagers dans les provinces voisines . . ."[1] What Pastoureau and René describe is true of the later tournament, but not so for the early years when the procedures were not quite as uniform. There is no question that the news of a tournament travelled far, yet in the mid-twelfth through the early-thirteenth centuries there were no prescribed instructions about its dissemination, certainly, heralds did little to help. The presence of heralds to proclaim tournaments was a role they gradually assumed, it was not a role they held at the onset of the sport. This is evidenced by the lack of stress on the heralds in the works upon whom the task of heralding the game would haven fallen.[2] Curiously, when in the rare times they are mentioned in early works, they play roles other than ones they will eventually acquire. For example, in *Le Maréchal*, a herald appears at a tournament at Joigni. When William is about to partake in the activities, the herald runs forth and asks for a good horse ("Mais el refreit out: "Mareschal / Kar me donez un bœn cheval!"" [vv. 3489–3490]). This wish is promptly granted, whereupon the herald goes off proudly with his new horse. The only thing he really announces is to have everyone look at his new possession, as he says: "Vez quel cheval! / C'est me dona le Mareschal" (vv. 3511–3512). The boy is referred to as an *héraut*, but in the work does not proclaim the tournament. The role he does assume is that of announcer and in this sense, herald, of William's generosity; he is a means through which William's reputation can be enhanced but has little to do with the contest itself.

If William appears to cultivate heralds in order to advance his own personal fame, he is not doing anything out of line for an ambitious knight of that era. But to what degree a herald is vocal about the achievements of a knight depends on the knight's existing reputation and his performance at any given moment. To wit, in *La Charrete*, aware of Lancelot's reputation, a herald runs about shouting out how wonderful he is (but not identifying Lancelot by name) before the start of the event. The herald is totally silent and speechless during the tournament when Lancelot is doing an abysmal job at competing. Later though, when Lancelot at last fights as best he can, and lives up to his pre-existing reputation, the herald cries out for all to hear that Lancelot will certainly win:

> Et li hyrauz se resbaudist
> tant qu'oiant toz cria et dist:
> "Or est venuz qui l'aunera!
> Huimés verroiz que il fera;
> Huimés aparra sa proesce!" (vv. 5961–5965)

Lancelot's marked improvement warrants publicity. His talent rather than lack of, deserves recognition, in fact, poorly talented or overly-confident knights are not to be publicly recognized. Even in *Yvain*, Chrétien remarks that heralds are eager to talk about worthy men, but say naught about braggarts ("Tant se teisent d'ax li hera, / qui des vaillanz crïent le banc / et les malvés gietent au vant" [vv. 2208–2210]).

Michel Stanesco contends that a fellow named Henri le Norrois was William Marshal's personal herald,[4] yet, there is no evidence during the event that Henri follows William around other than from pure devotion. The same can be said for essentially all the works; there is no evidence that any man has the role of an *héraut* as it is better known. And while there is no concrete evidence in the works that any certain herald is under the employ of any particular knight, there are frequent references to squires; Cligés in fact, has at least three ("Trois de ses escuiers aler" [*Cligés*, v. 4550]). Knights are consistently identified with their own personal squires,[5] but not with their own heralds.

In the absence of heralds announcing the tournament, the authors must use other means to relay that a tournament is imminent; they do so through certain expressions in which some sort of "heralding" is inherent: "summens" (*Ipomedon*), "feront savoir et crïer" (*La Charrete*), "aporté(e) la parole" and "refist grant parole" (*Le Maréchal*). Noticeably, these expressions are quite neutral, provoke little excitement, and tend to have no explicit subject. One assumes that the subject is a herald but none is mentioned. In the romance *La Charrete*, the news of a tournament 'goes,' 'is said,' and 'is told' ("Tant est par le rëaume alee / la novele, dite et contee" [vv. 5423–5424]). The three short verbs advance the action quickly enough to lend a bit of importance to the announcement, but the verbs *alee*, *dite* and *contee* are in the passive voice, with no stated agent.

Marie de France does not explicitly mention any heralds in her *lais*; she tends to state in brief phrases, also in which heralding is implicit, that a tournament is to occur. For example, in "Guigemar" she writes: "e ci qu'a un turneiement / Que Merïadus afia" (vv. 743–744). In "Milun" she notes that the men will assemble together ("Al Munt Seint Michel s'asemblerent" [v. 385]). In "Chaitivel" a scheduled tournament is 'shouted out' ("ot un turnoiement crié" [v. 74]). In *Cligés*, Chrétien says that Cligés' men are informed of a prospective tournament, "reconté lor fu" (v. 4539). In *Amadas et Ydoine*, companions are "invited" (*mandés*)[6] to a tournament, but we cannot be sure as to what formalities comprised this "invited" since not a one is mentioned in the text. The news of another tournament is not explicitly announced; one learns of it by hearing that it was "undertaken" ("Mais oï a c'avoient pris" [v. 1562]). In no case from *Amadas et Ydoine* is a herald actually shown to proclaim the tournament, but in one passage there is an allusion to the customs of which Pastoureau spoke. In this passage, a young boy tells Amadas that he is carrying messages to all his master's friends in the area to tell them about the upcoming event ("Ci environ par cest païs / port letres a ses amis" [vv. 4093–4094]). The boy is a servant though, and not an *héraut*. Any invitations suggested or alluded to in the works are not elaborate like the ones René d'Anjou paints in his book. The proclamation of a tournament through a herald, in the period in question, is a relatively minor detail and the conclusion is evident that heralds were not yet as important as they were to become.

The length of time a knight had to wait between the announcement and the actual beginning of a tournament served a purpose for the knights and the authors as well. An author of purely fictional narrative had the convenience of varying the wait to achieve different effects. Occasionally, the wait creates a remarkable tension in the hero's life; other times it merely serves to allow participants time to receive the news and in turn arrive at the place of action. A long waiting period can be a cunning tactic to allow increased numbers to compete. In some regards, the waiting is nothing more than an implicit detail.

The waiting period before a tournament was normally two to three weeks: Tournaments 1 and 6 in *Le Maréchal*, "E por ce fu mis a quinzeine" (v. 1207), and "A treis semeines a Pleierre" (v. 2879). Similarly in *Cligés*: "Car plus de quinze jorz antiers" (v. 4550). And while the two-to-three-week time frame was the norm, there was considerable fluctuation. For example, certain participants do not even have to wait: one day in *Le Maréchal*, William and the Young King come across a place where a tournament is being held (vv. 2577–2636), and they immediately join the fracas and compete. This particular scene indicates that such events were constantly taking place in the late twelfth century. They were so frequent even someone such as William, who made it his business to keep informed about when and where the next tournament would be held, could not keep up with all of them. Tournaments were so commonplace that knights often chanced upon them on journeys. This particular tournament also reveals that knights did not have to register beforehand and could enter whenever or wherever they wished, an element supported in several fictional works, one of which is *Perceval*. The tournament in which Gawain eventually competes has been arranged before his arrival and begins just after he arrives. He, however, has not travelled to Tintaguel for the sport, in fact, he is not aware of it until after he arrives. Even though Gawain knows nothing about the event prior to his arrival, when he agrees to compete, there is no opposition to his doing so.

Elsewhere, as in *Partonopeus de Blois*, the knights must wait a full year for the tournament. The long duration of a year's wait before the tournament gives the author ample time in which he can manipulate his hero's life. His hero must travel far, as well as overcome several obstacles during the waiting period. During the year, Partonopeus: learns of the tournament, is located and equipped by two maidens, taken by these same maidens to the land of the tournament, in turn captured, granted temporary freedom to leave, and finally, travels to the site of the event to compete. Decidedly, a year was necessary for Partonopeus.

In *La Charrete*, we are told that the tournament will be held a "long time" from its announcement, but there is no indication just how long: "et firent a molt lonc termine / crïer le jor de l'ahatine" (vv. 5377–5378). The idea here of a long wait enables more people to attend, and this is duly noted by the author: "por ce que plus i eüst genz" (v. 5379). A greater number of participants will not only render the event more illustrious, but also allow the maidens who have organized it, to have a wider selection of men from which to choose a spouse. Furthermore, there needs to be plenty of time for the news to reach Lancelot, who is being held captive. In this regard, the news itself goes on a quest to find Lancelot, and with a window of a "long time" the news has a good chance of reaching Lancelot before the game begins and ends.

In *Ipomedon*, waiting for the tournament will take four months ("A quatre meis asist le jur" [v. 2568]). The four-month waiting period in *Ipomedon* serves a function similar to that of the long wait in *La Charrete*. The tournament is to be held in a distant land and the news must travel far to reach the hero, and, subsequently, give him (and other participants) reasonable time to travel to the arena of competition. This delay, however, does more than simply allow sufficient time for travel. It also enables Ipomedon to perfect a masquerade. Owing to the long waiting period, he is able to convince everyone that he is nothing but a hunter, and a cowardly one at that. He uses the long wait to his own advantage and manipulates the people around him into believing what he wants.

In *Amadas et Ydoine*, the hero must wait forty days for an expected tournament ("Et doit estre a quarante jours" [v. 1565]). These forty days help to build the excitement for the event. Although the verses composing this passage are no more than twenty, the author creates a great sense of anticipation by the mention of "quarante jours." In fact, as the author points out, this long wait tests the patience of the hero, Amadas ("Si vous di bien que lons sejors / Li couste mult de grant mesure" [vv. 1566–1567]), and demoralizes him because he is so terribly anxious to compete and cannot bear the thought of waiting ("La demourance le dechut [v. 1573]). Unfortunately for Amadas, because he had so greatly anticipated the tournament, hoping surely to distinguish himself there, he is sorely disappointed when it is eventually postponed (although truly it is cancelled since it never takes place):

> Remés est li tournoiemens
> Dont Amadas est mult dolens
> Car mult se quidoit aloser
> Le jor par les armes porter. (vv. 1587–1590)

The tournament had been scheduled for forty days, but on the day it is to be held, ("Quant vint au jor que estre dut" [v. 1574]), the King of France forbids it because he fears that a real war will ensue whilst it is supposed to be a friendly competition.

Despite the cancellation of this tournament, Amadas has the opportunity to distinguish himself at another one later in the romance. Concerning this one, Amadas has only an eight-day wait from the time he learns of it to its beginning. Amadas, however, is in Lucca, Italy which, conveniently, is in the region of the event; therefore the eight days notice is plenty of time to find a horse and get properly dressed and equipped. He obtains what he needs, and leaves Lucca two days before the tournament. As the narrator points out, Amadas is so near the tourneying field, that he does not have to rush, and rather ambles along:

> Qu'il n'a pas a errer granment
> Jusqu'au liu u il doit aler
> Ains que venist a l'avesprer
> I vint la petit ambleüre,
> Com cil qui aps ne s'aseüre. (vv. 4242–4246)

Unlike William Marshal who frequently has to rush, Amadas has no problem with time; and by the way, nor does Cligés in his romance.

In *Cligés*, the two-week time period is mentioned in order to show how the hero has an opportunity to orient himself in Britain, seeing how he has just arrived from Constantinople. The fortnight allows him to get prepared at a calm pace, and not worry since he has fifteen days:

> Mes ainz porroit molt sejourner
> Cligés, por son cors atorner,
> Se rien li faut endemantiers

Car plus de quinze jorz antiers
Avoit jusqu'au tornoiemant. (vv. 4547–4551)

Although not always avoidable, it is wise for a knight not to rush. When he has ample time he can gather his thoughts and prepare himself well; we see that this is precisely the case for Cligés.

Chrétien de Troyes does not directly speak of the waiting period in *Perceval* or *Erec et Enide*; as mentioned, there is no wait before the start of the tournament in *Perceval*. In *Erec et Enide*, the reader must calculate the amount of time before the event. During the third week of the wedding celebration, a tournament is agreed upon by "all" ("tuit ansanble comunemant / anpristrent un tornoiemant" [vv. 2089–2090]). Seven lines later, the time at which the tournament is to be held is given: "Un mois aprés la Pantecoste / li tornoiz assanble et ajoste" (vv. 2097–2098). One has to go back to lines 1891 and 1892 to determine that the wedding took place at Pentecost. If the celebrations went on for three weeks after Pentecost, and the tournament was held one month afterward, then the waiting period is approximately one week. This brief mathematical exercise is relevant because it shows that the waiting period is of little significance to this tale. Unlike in *Ipomedon* or *Partonopeus de Blois*, there are no apparent obstacles or dilemmas for the hero prior to the commencement and thus, the author does not bother making the wait explicit.

Likewise, Marie de France does not mention how long a knight must wait for an upcoming tournament because it is not important to the anticipation she has already created in her *lais*. In "Chaitivel" the reason for the tournament creates the suspense. In "Milun" the knowledge that Milun is going to meet his dreaded adversary creates a similar high level of anticipation and suspense. In "Guigemar" the fact that the antagonist, Merïadus, is to hold a tournament lends excitement to the tale. The waiting period itself, is of minor significance to each of Marie's *lais*, certainly, of not enough importance actually to mention to any great detail.

Through the sources, it is clear that tourneying was such a popular sport it occurred quite regularly from spring to fall.[7] In *Le Maréchal*, the author complains that he cannot possibly list all the tournaments in which William entered because they were held almost every fifteen days, ergo, too numerous to count:

De trestoz les tornei[e]menz.
L'om les savreit a molt grant peine,

Quer près de chascune quinze[i]ne
Torneieut l'om de place en place. (vv. 4972–4975)

Paradoxically, this frequency of tournaments which requires a knight to move from one place to another, provides a relatively stable occupation for some; it was, after all, William's profession for about ten years. Amadas too, wanders around Europe going from tournament to tournament. He is able to find enough tournaments to "wander and tourney" for three years:

Tant a erré de tere en tere
La ou il seut tournoi ne guerre,
Trois ans entiers cerke son pris
Noblement par pluseurs païs. (vv. 1431–1434)

Amadas has no other identified means of support during these years.

Even though tournaments were much enjoyed, there was a limited time during the year in which they took place; they were typically held around the same time in spring, in part, because of the Catholic liturgical cycle. Lent was to be a time of penance and a time of truce from pugilistic endeavors, therefore, no tournaments were to be held then. Not until the end of Easter, or Pentecost, were tournaments typically scheduled. Marie mentions in "Milun" that a whole winter having passed, tournaments, wars, and battles began again at Eastertime: "Desques aprés la Paske vint, / K'il recumencent les turneiz / E les gueres e les dereiz" (vv. 382–384). References in other works to these same times of year include: "Tant qu'aprés une Paske vint" ("Chaitivel," v. 71), "un mois aprés la Pantecoste" (Erec et Enide, v. 2097), "De la Penteste en un an" (Partonopeus de Blois, v. 6547), and "As oytaves de Pentecoste" (Le Maréchal, v. 3683). Curiously, while spring was the preferred season for many reasons, there is one example in Le Maréchal where the tournament takes place in the winter: "Al vintisme jor de Noël" (v. 5974). One can only imagine how cold the weather must have been. Winter though, is not an ideal and common time for the event.

Spring would naturally be the season of choice given its habitual temperate weather; spring also gives rise to psychological factors of ambition and rejuvenation. The author of Amadas et Ydoine takes care to reflect, quite extensively, on the positive effects of spring and its pleasant conditions which foster thoughts of honor and fame i.e., participation in tourneying:

En leur ostel ou tans Pascours,
Quant li tans est et clers et biaus
Et retentist li cans d'oisiaus,
Que la saison par grant douçour
Recommuet tout de grant baudor
Et remaine en joliveté
Les jovenes gens qui ont amé
Et qui aiment houneur et pris
Li tans fu haus, ce m'est avis,
Et biaus et caus comme en esté. (vv. 4020–4029)

The author's elaboration on the sights, sounds, and effects of spring in the above passage are not his only appreciation of the good weather because he mentions it again a bit further: "Et li tans noviaus et jolis" (v. 4226). Pleasant spring weather is like a balm for Amadas, and brings him a sweet sense of calm: "Li ramentoit les grans douçors / Et le deduit de ses amors" (vv. 4227–4228). In such apparent reverence for the season, we see a touch of sensitivity in the poet as well as in Amadas, but the emphasis also serves to parallel Amadas' life with the lifecycle of springtime. As we shall see in another chapter, at this point, Amadas is starting over, or being reborn again.

The poets of the purely fictional works have taken a literary license in occasionally adapting the announcement and waiting period to the needs of their narrative and their hero. While their special treatment of aspects, for example in creating a long wait before a tournament for the convenience of the hero, may enhance the suspense, at the same time, it lends a certain importance to these two often overlooked elements of the sport.

Notes

1. Pastoureau, 135.

2. As Anthony Wagner points out "they were sent beforehand to proclaim tournaments." Anthony Wagner, *Heralds and Heraldry in the Middle Ages* (Oxford: Oxford University Press, 1939), 25.

3. "Après tout, si le Maréchal avait quelque peu recherché la faveur des jongleurs ou des hérauts d'armes, il n'aurait fait que suivre l'exemple des seigneurs de son temps soucieux de leur réputation. Les hérauts étaient les journalistes de l'époque, et il pouvait être avantageux de se concilier leurs bonnes grâces." Meyer, *Le Maréchal* vol. 3, xlv.

4. Stanesco, 184.

5. "The *esquire* or armour-bearer, was the immediate attendant of a knight . . . ," Andrew Bell, *A History of Feudalism British and Continental* (London: Longman, Green, Longman, Roberts, & Green, 1863), 78.

6. *Amadas et Ydoine*, trans. Jean-Claude Aubailly (Paris: Honoré Champion, 1986). This is Aubailly's translation into modern French, p. 28.

7. ". . . on en organise tous les quinze jours, de février à novembre, ..." Pastoureau, 134.

Chapter IV

Opening and Closing Procedures

The opening and closing of the early tournament did not generally involve extensive ceremony, although there were some traditions present and forming what would later evolve into great pomp and circumstance. The former were frequently referred to as *començailles* or *vespres*, the latter were sometimes called *parlements*.

The opening exercises are the more problematic of the two because of the two terms *començailles* and *vespres*, which seem to be used interchangeably. In the tournament at Gournei and Ressons in *Le Maréchal*, these exercises are called *començailles* ("Poi durérent les començailles" [v. 6057]). Earlier in the same work, the poet had referred to such preliminaries as *vespres* ("Comenciérent molt asprement / Les vespres del torneiemant" [vv. 3709–3710]). Whichever word an author chose, they were all the same, pre-tournament skirmishes "in which individual knights fought together before their companies joined in the action."[1] That vespers were pre-tournament pugilistic engagements is corroborated in Marie de France's "Chaitivel," when after knights had fought hard at vespers, the tournament began. However, this was not a moment where any participant could join in the fracas. The procedure at hand was delegated to men in the employ of barons or of other great men; the barons preferred to send out their men (*lor genz*) during these opening exercises instead of engaging in the exercises themselves: "Que li baron e li halt home / As vespres pas ne torneiérent / Mais de lor genz i enveiérent" (*Le Maréchal*, vv. 3716–3718). The middle line of this example is revealing because it reinforces the notion that during this specific moment in the event, the barons and great men did not tourney (*pas ne torneiérent*). In *Partonopeus de Blois*, the same is true on the second day of the tournament when the barons also send out their men first ("Puis sont

armé, vont al tornoi, / lor gent envoient avant soi" [vv. 8289–8290]).
Apparently, the opening skirmishes were not ones sought out by the
barons because they were brief, little was to gain from them, and they
were hard fought ("al vespre del turneiement / s'entreferirent durement"
["Chaitivel," vv. 83–84]). These skirmishes could injure someone so
decisively that further participation in the subsequent showcase tournament might be impossible.

If, then, the barons did not venture out, who were exactly *lor genz*?
It appears that the *genz* were rookie knights; typically the newly-dubbed
or "green" knights.[2] Evidence of this appears in words that express
inexperience, for example, certain adjectives such as "young": "Li
giemble home si com il durent" (*Le Maréchal*, v. 3708). While it is
true that the inexperience of those knights who partake of the pre-
tournament action is not always indicated, it seems highly unlikely that
a well-established baron-knight would turn down the chance of a
començaille if it were an important establishment of talent.

The poets clearly make the term "vespers" synonymous with
començailles, and this is where problems arise. The term "vespers"
presents a problem in that the term, even contemporaneously, meant
two things in connection with the tournament; the pre-tournament
skirmishes already identified, and the end of the available daylight. It is
further complicated because vespers had a third meaning in the daily
life of the everyday people. Initially, in daily life, vespers referred to
one of the liturgical hours of prayer;[3] it normally occurred in late after-
noon. The association of vespers with the end of the day in daily life
is thus understandable. However, when used in the context of the end
of the day during a tournament scene, vespers have no religious connotations as in "Vespres estoit, retorné sont" (*Amadas et Ydoine*, v.
4551) or in *Erec et Enide*: "les vespres sonerent a tant" (v. 2214).
Admittedly, the verb *sonerent* in line 2214 indicates a ringing of bells,
hence, an association with the church is possible, but this "ringing" is
more likely merely a means to indicate audibly the time of day[4] for the
knights and one did not necessarily have to go pray. Vespers signaled
the end of the day, generally when the daylight was diminishing. The
tournament ends when there is no more daylight, not because vespers
as prayers have arrived. Decidedly, when the term "vespers" is used as
a synonym for nightfall in a tournament scene, there is little, if any,
religious indication. In the daily life, the term did have religious meaning, but it is not the case when the term is used in conjunction with the
sport. The ecclesiastical term was used in the works because it had

become a standard indication of time. The precise interpretation of the term in a text oftentimes is difficult but a bit easier to understand when the possibilities are given.

There was on occasion another tradition before the tournament, but it was not part of the action itself and was more of a social tradition. The night before the event, knights ventured out to visit their peers in the towns:

> Li halt home qui s'i esmueent
> Par[mi] la vile esbergié furent,
> E s[i] est costome qu'al seir
> Vont li un les autres v[e]eir
> A lor ostels: c'est beals usages. (*Le Maréchal*, vv. 4329–4333)

With the use of "it is customary at night" (*est costome qu'al seir*), the author of the biographical narrative depicts such nocturnal events as a frequent occurrence but they have no particular name. These gatherings on the eve of a competition reinforce the notion that knights were part of a fraternity which could get along well; many were good friends off the field.

The end of a tournament as well, involved certain traditions. As has been shown, the contest most often ended with the advent of nightfall. What could follow the competition were also gatherings of the participants which came to be known as *parlements*. It is a time to talk and to discuss the day's events. There are several references to this practice in *Le Maréchal*, as in Tournament 6 at Pleurs; when the tournament is over, some men inquire about friends or relatives:

> E li autre molt enqueroient
> As plusors del tornei[e]ment,
> S'il oïssent aveiement
> De lor parenz, de lor amis,
> S'il savoient quis aveit pris. (vv. 3024–3028)

After the tournament at Eu, Tournament 7, once again the author notes the combatants get together to talk:

> Tuit li haut home, ce me semble,
> Kar parler voloient ensemble.
> Entor le rei s'atropelérent
> Tuit li haut home qui la érent.
> Si parlérent de me[i]nt afeire
> Si comme en tel lieu estuet faire. (vv. 3303–3308)

The practice is becoming customary or so the poet suggests with the line 3308 above, "As it was done in this place." In Tournament 14, as the poet notes, the important men gather together to talk: "Li halt home, si com mei semble, / E que il parlassent ensemble" (vv. 5599–5600). The tradition is not referred to specifically as a *parlement* up to this point in the work, although the verb *parler* is used in some form. It is not until Tournament 15 that this type of reunion is actually called a *parlement*: "Li halt home, al departement / Vindrent asemble al parlement / En la place ou il torneiérent" (vv. 6147–6149).

In the romance *La Charrete*, *parlements* are inferred when after the first day of combat, the knights talk about who had fought the best that day ("Au departir i ot grant plet / de ces qui mialz l'avoient fet" [vv. 5707–5708]). The tradition of *parlements*, however, was not yet all-important, so it is not as evident in other sources. It is true that the scenes after the tournament in the romance *Ipomedon* tell of meetings, but they are not exclusively between groups of knights. The meetings are among various people, be they the knights or the Queen and others. Therein, scenes show how interested the Queen and *la Fiere* are and how they wish to know who won the day's fighting. Much of the interlude between each day's competition, is spent showing how the king and everyone search in vain for the mysterious knight's identity, and although the tournament is an engaging dinner topic, there are no references to particular customs such as *parlements* devoted solely to the men. In *Partonopeus de Blois*, the judges are shown to be discussing the tournament, but they do so to choose the victor and this is hardly the same as a *parlement*. In *Cligés*, the night before each day's events, the men find each other and talk, but these meetings are not referred to as customary or with a specific term, even though they fit the loose definition of a *parlement*. Despite the rarity of their appearance, the absence of *parlements* in many of the sources should not negate the importance that they were acquiring. The inconsistency of their appearance should be a reflection of the ever-evolving nature of the sport and its trappings.

While the closing of a tournament is described in varying verse length, stylistically, the phrases are all quite similar: "E li tornoiemenz depart" (*Perceval*, v. 5528), "L'anhatine ensi departi" (*La Charrete*, v. 6055), "Li turneiz a espleit s'en part" (*Ipomedon*, v. 6295), "Quant li turneiemenz depart" ("Milun," v. 481), "Li tornei[e]menz departi" (*Le Maréchal*, v. 5045), "Si se vait chascuns de sa part / E li torneieme[n]z depart" (*Le Maréchal*, vv. 6141–6142), and "Atant est partis li tornois" (*Partonopeus de Blois*, v. 8235). The closure of the tournament can arrive abruptly or can be drawn out to great lengths. In general though, when the tournament has ended there is not much lingering on the field. The knights leave to partake of another activity—occasionally a *parlement*. There is little to portend the end of a tournament. No time limit is set except for the end of daylight, which really proves to be the most deciding factor for closure. There is not a visible goal or number of points which has to be reached. The men tourney until it seems one team or even a single knight has taken all adversaries or when one team has proven itself better. As such, the manner in which the poets close the passage can be as sudden as when night finally falls.

A literary technique employed by the poets, is that on occasion they include interesting anecdotes that occur after each engagement. For example, in *Ipomedon*, the author spends time recreating the confusion over the mysterious knight's identity and the anxiety experienced by *la Fiere pucele*. In *Le Maréchal*, there are little episodes, peripheral to the tournament but pertinent to the subject William Marshal. Such anecdotes are a subtle feature, but often a vital one to the narrative's subject.

In conclusion, the early tournament did not generally experience a specific and consistent ceremony to open or close the event as the later days of the sport did. The notion of *començailles* or *parlements* was surely a precursor to later grander traditions, but while they play a part in the tournament theater from an early age, they are not afforded as high a degree of attention as some of the other aspects of the event. This is no doubt due to their unassuming nature in the early stages of the game's development. All the same, the rare glimpses of what opening and closing procedures could be help visualize the whole affair.

Notes

1. Barker, *The Tournament*, 141.

2. "Nous découvrons que ces engagements préliminaires sont habituellement réservés aux débutants." Philippe Ménard, "Les Vespres del tournoiement," in *Miscellanea di Studi Romanzi offerta a Guiliano Gasca Queirazza per suo 65o compleanno* (Torino: Edizioni Dell'Orso, 1988), 651–662, 654.

3. See Paul Lacroix's, *Military and Religious Life in the Middle Ages and the Renaissance* (New York: Frederick Ungar, 1964), Chapter 7 ("Liturgy and Ceremonies") for a good discussion on divisions of the day.

4. "For the vast majority of people in medieval France the sole means of reckoning time was by the sun and the canonical hours." W. Rothwell, "The Hours of the Day in Medieval French," *French Studies* XIII, 3 (July 1959): 240–51; 243.

Chapter V

Who Were the Participants?

It is well known that most men who competed in a medieval tournament were knights; the majority of which are consistently portrayed as good, loyal, brave, generous, and bestowed with the best qualities found in mankind. It is less well known, however, that when literary accounts of the tournaments are viewed more extensively, many men are associated with lifestyles or past incidents which do not readily fit into the paradigm of "chivalry." A mutual social standing afforded knights access to a particular society, yet aside from this elite society those who compete represent a diverse group of men. This is precisely the case in the early medieval works where competitors are richly developed and complicated since they include masqueraders who carefully prepare the scene that they wish to act out at the tournament, prisoners, and in one narrative, a cured madman. There is one hero who is an adulterer; there are fathers, husbands, bachelors, and duped lovers. On a hierarchic class level, men of humble origin as well as aristocrats and members of royalty compete. There are historical as well as fictional characters; some are old, others young. There are knights whose names alone evoke the highest ideals of chivalry, others whose names do just the opposite, and still others who remain anonymous.

The participants are affected publicly and personally by the tournament in a variety of ways. Sometimes norms are reversed if only temporarily; on occasion, whole lives may turn around permanently as the result of a tournament. The knights compete for a myriad of reasons, quite a few of which are: livelihood, defense of the honor of a maiden (*pucelle*), reputation, destruction of an enemy, acquisition of a precious prize, expression of political affiliations, and last, but not least, love. Some knights continue a family tradition by tourneying;

and, the participants represent a number of regional alliances and
nationalities. With all these features, it is of interest and value to view
those who compete more closely.

Several knights who participate do so under various guises, inten-
tional or not. Three knights in this category who quite deliberately
keep their identity hidden are Ipomedon, Cligés, and Lancelot.
Ipomedon, in the romance bearing his name, learns of the tournament that is to be held four months hence in Calabria. He obviously
feels that a specific public opinion of his character is a necessary element to his pre-meditated masquerade and so travels to Calabria those
months prior to the event. Once there, Ipomedon becomes a servant
(*dru*) to the Queen and rather a "fool" at the royal court in order to
persuade everyone he cares not in the least for tournaments. In fact,
publicly, he appears to lose all interest in tourneying and will not even
carry on a conversation with other knights about the sport. While
they speak of knightly deeds and tournaments, he speaks of hunting
and dogs:

> Quant il cuntent chevaleries
> Il recounte de veneries,
> Cil parolent de forz esturz
> E il brachetz e de ostourz,
> Cil cuntent de turneemenz
> E il de chens, igneaus e lenz,
> Cil cuntent de bon chevaliers,
> Il de veautres e de levrers. (vv. 3111–3118)

Then when the tournament begins each of the three days, he goes
into the woods ostensibly to hunt wild animals. Once out of view he
puts on his equipment and then in guise returns to the playing field.
He does this each day and thus appears as three different knights
who, not surprisingly, best all others. In order to thwart suspicion, his
dupery continues in the evenings when he discusses his hunting endeavors, convincing all he is merely a meek hunter. Naturally, since he
acts as though he cares little for the sport of tourneying, no one expects him even to participate in the imminent tournament, certainly
not to win it. Ipomedon is so successful with his performance that no
one suspects the multiple roles he has assumed until the truth is revealed at the close of the whole event.

Whereas Ipomedon masquerades as three separate knights, Cligés,
the eponymous hero, appears as four different knights during the four-
day tournament. Just as Ipomedon did, Cligés decides aforehand to

compete without revealing his true identity. His plan is in part successful because he hails from Constantinople and is essentially unknown to the men of Britain. He is, furthermore, aided in maintaining his anonymity by the different equipment he uses each day. He carefully plans his scheme first by taking four different horses with him on his journey to Britain. After arriving, he sends out his squires to procure three more sets of armor to add to the one he already has. Unlike Ipomedon, he does not have to act cowardly in public prior to the event, but he must not wear any recognizable family emblems. As might be expected, being the hero of the romance, Cligés physically outshines most of the knights[1] of King Arthur on the playing field. Although Cligés' decision could be interpreted as arrogant, he is just the opposite, and in fact, once his identity is revealed, he is rather embarrassed by all the attention he receives ("Car plus le oent tuit ansanble / Que il ne voldroit, ce li sanble; / Mes bel li est, si en a honte" [vv. 4961–4963]). Cligés chooses to prove his prowess while disguised precisely because he is the nephew of Sir Gawain and a removed nephew of King Arthur and does not want false accolades based on his bloodline. Cligés is a portrait of a humble, yet worthy knight, and is subsequently highly regarded.

Lancelot is the third mentioned knight who appears at a tournament in disguise. His case differs slightly from those already seen because his anonymity is intitially unintentional by way of borrowing someone else's armor and equipment. Yet, for reasons not explicitly stated, he does choose to maintain the secrecy surrounding him as best as possible. He too, masquerades and assumes the role of an actor because during the tournament he performs according to someone else's (Queen Guinevere) directions and wishes rather than his own. Lancelot is adept at remaining mysterious and everyone wonders who he is. He is good even to the extent that one of his best friends does not recognize him. However, unlike Ipomedon and Cligés who succeed completely with their masquerades until they choose to unmask, Lancelot is not able to conceal his identity from everyone, and two people figure out who he is but keep his secret. For Lancelot, this recognition, at least by one person, is necessary because it establishes the basis for his performance at the tournament.

Partonopeus de Blois, also competes in a tournament where he is not recognized because he too is wearing borrowed fittings. Contrary to Lancelot, Ipomedon, and Cligés, though, Partonopeus does not intentionally maintain his anonymity, he just does not seem to find the time or the appropriate moment to reveal his identity. He is not expected at the event, and he is not wearing any personal emblems to be recognized, so his beloved does not even suspect he is actually there. Only at the end of the competition is his identity revealed.

The fact that these knights prefer, for their own various reasons, not to be recognized is certainly uncharacteristic of most knights for whom recognition is a vital dimension of the chivalric realm. However, there is no sense of rebuke in the narration and as such, none of the heroes does anything unethical by competing in disguise. Although it is out of the ordinary, masquerading is a perfectly plausible means of participation, and is not damaging to a knight's reputation.

Lancelot and Partonopeus in their respective romances, do compete anonymously, yet, besides the mystery which surrounds them throughout the action, their characters are further developed because they are, in addition, prisoners. In their stories, each hero is being held captive but manages to receive news of the upcoming tournament. Coincidently, their respective jailkeepers happen to be gone when the news arrives, and they both succeed at obtaining permission from the wives of the jailkeepers to compete provided they return immediately to the prison at the event's conclusion. On the surface their presence at the tournament appears to be similar to any other—that of a knight, free to compete. All the same, underneath such an appearance of freedom and homogeny, they contrast with their peers since they are prisoners.

A knight's personal life was in many ways intertwined with his life of chivalry, yet did not necessarily interfere with his public one. Both lives co-exist well enough that a "tainted" or checkered past does not prevent a knight from tourneying, not even if it includes insanity. For example, in *Amadas et Ydoine*, Amadas for a time, goes completely mad ("un fol dervé" v. 2711); destitute and crazed to the point where he is filthy, naked, and bouncing about like a squirrel in the streets:

> Amadas trestout nu venir,
> Tous déguisés, en crins tondus,
> Com cil qui a le sens perdus. . .
> Mult durement est ors et sales. . .
> Les menus saus, plus qu'escureus,
> S'en va la rue contreval. (vv. 2722–2759)

He has reached the depths of disgrace, but fortunately, he is found and rehabilitated, learning to walk, eat, and talk again. He is above all, a knight who can overcome adversity, and thus is able to transcend his illness. The year-long mental lapse in his personal life does not deter Amadas from reviving his former chivalric lifestyle. He eventually competes in a tournament and is the victor, once again a knight all others wish to follow and emulate.

Duplicity and insanity did not disqualify a knight from participating nor did illicit love relationships. The knight in question is Guigemar who, in the *lai* of the same name, is a so-called adulterer since he has secret encounters with the wife of a very old man ("Ensemble gisent e parolent / E souvent baisent e acolent" [vv. 531–532]). Considering, however, the nasty portrait of the old husband in the *lai*, and the professed sincere love Guigemar and the lady have for each other, their affair seems natural. He has acted out of true love, and so Guigemar is still a knight worthy of competing in a tournament. His personal life has little or no affect on his public, knightly life, and he accepts to compete when he is later invited to a tournament ("Il li manda par gueredun" [v. 749]).

Other types of participants in the literary tournament include a young son and his unwed, ageing father Milun in the *lai* of the same name, and the husband Erec in *Erec et Enide*, all of whom, as a literary technique, establish contrasts in the narratives. In "Milun," the contrasts are obvious with the father and son, young versus old. In *Erec et Enide*, the notion that Erec is married is a contrast because, while celibacy is not a prerequisite to knighthood or to tourneying, most competitive knights are unmarried. The fierce nature of the sport, and the absences it would require from a stable family life contribute to the reasons most knights were still bachelors. In the *lai* "Chaitivel," the status of the four main characters in the competition is extended beyond that of mere knights inasmuch as they are duped lovers. They are tricked because each one loves the lady responsible for the tournament without knowing she is courting the other three.[2] The secondary condition as duped lovers ends up being an important factor because it indirectly affects the outcome of the narrative.

Men from humble beginnings, such as William Marshal, compete in tournaments, as well as aristocrats and royalty.[3] While the participation of royalty in a tournament is regarded as a boost to its fame and much appreciated, the author of *Le Maréchal* takes care to assert that royalty's appearance is not always necessary for a good performance. In the following example, the contest at Lagni sur Marne is going very well even before the king and count enter into it: "Molt fu li

torn[e]i[e]menz buens / Anceis que li reis ne li quens / I venissent por
asembler" (vv. 4817–4819). Nonetheless, in the sixteen tournaments
described by the poet of the biography, approximately half are attended by members of royalty, be it the son of Henry II of England,
who is a frequent participant, or royalty from other territories such as
William the Lion, the King of Scotland. In *Partonopeus de Blois* there
are twenty-five kings from various lands who compete; in the story of
Cligés, the hero himself is of royal lineage, and in the same story, King
Arthur seems to approve of the event since he has allowed it to take
place.

Decidedly, the bans seem not to have scared away aristocrats, and
the sport was cultivated by the wealthy and socially prominent. In *Le
Maréchal*, dukes, counts, and noble men are ever-present, for example, the Count of Saint Pol and the Duke of Burgundy are participants on occasion; frequently the author notes there were "Maint duc,
maint conte, maint halt home" (v. 5979). In Tournament 12, there are
nineteen counts and one duke in addition to the Young King. In *Cligés*,
the grandest of the barons in the land are present ("Tuit le haut baron
de la terre" [v. 4579]). At first the inclusion of the upper echelons in
the sport may not seem unusual, but it rather is when one considers
that it was banned so early by the Catholic Church, and by some royal
houses. Yet, it is important to list such elite participants in order to
demonstrate the aristocratic nature of the tournament, and to show
that, though so condemned, tournaments enjoyed official approval in
some parts of Europe, France in particular. The list of such illustrious
competitors is also necessary to the literature because it is a fact that
nobles competed and thus adds an element of veracity to the narratives.

The social status of the participants gives light to one of the more
interesting facets of the tournament for it is during the performance
that the normal differences between classes are eliminated. Men who
in daily life are mere[4] knights, suddenly find themselves in the same
situation and on the same or an even superior level as a king or a
duke. In *Le Maréchal*, at first glance, the tournaments in which the
Young King and William are together reveal few physical and mental
differences between the two. They are two young men striving to
maneuver their arms as well as possible. Yet, in truth, William emerges
as the Young King's superior, at least in military prowess. According
to the author, early in William's career, he leads the Young King all
over the land seeking out tournaments in order to teach the Young
King the art of tourneying: "Cil le mena par meinte terre, / qui bien le
saveit avei[e]r, / La ou l'en deveit torn[e]ier" (vv. 1960–1962). The

young king Henry is apparently not terribly adept at tourneying, and
he and his team (*mesnie*) are often defeated during an event. It is not
until William begins his tutelage and remains by young Henry's side
that the latter is no longer defeated each time they venture to compete. Young Henry's successes are not entirely because of the acquired teachings, rather it is due to William himself. Most assuredly,
the presence of William next to the royal heir is so intimidating that
no opponent dares strike at the Young King for fear of being bopped
by the Marshal:

> Nuls n'i osout tendre la main
> Por li haper ne prendre al frein
> Por les granz cops al Mareschal
> Qui trop érent pesant e mal. (vv. 2615–2618)

Young Henry's team is able to win in all encounters as long as William
rides side by side with him.[5] Although in social standing the royal heir
is far superior to William, in tournament matters it is the other way
around and hierarchic social orders are reversed with no shame afforded the displaced royal.

Duly noted, the social status of participants can be affected during
a tournament; in *La Charrete*, Chrétien de Troyes reverses other orders. Under normal circumstances, a knight entered a tournament to
defeat and capture prisoners, clearly identifying himself for reasons of
reputation. Instead, Lancelot enters as a prisoner, captures no one,
and leaves as an unknown knight. Typically, knights competed in order to do their best, to show how talented they were. Contrary to this,
Lancelot does his absolute worst most of the first day and during part
of the second. Admittedly, he fights so poorly only because he is obeying
the orders of the Queen; nevertheless, the effect is the same. Lancelot
completely befuddles the spectators, who first ridicule him unmerci-
fully and then have to recant when he does well:

> Et cil qui gaber le soloient
> dïent: "Honi somes et mort.
> Molt avomes eü grant tort
> de lui despire et avillier.
> Certes il valt bien un millier
> de tex a en cest chanp assez. (vv. 5984–5989)

Partonopeus, in his own story, competes as a prisoner, who, like
Lancelot, is granted temporary freedom; yet, unlike Lancelot, he does
not have to perform poorly. For Partonopeus then, the only real rever-
sal is that he is a prisoner while competing rather than a true freeman.

Many of these same knights can be identified further as historical or fictitious figures, well-known or relatively obscure. In several fictional works there are various characters not readily associated with King Arthur and his realm, to wit, Amadas. Characteristically, the knights who participate in the tournaments in the romances of Chrétien de Troyes are legendary[6] figures of the Arthurian tradition. These are the Knights of the Round Table, such as Perceval, Gawain, Lancelot, and Cligés, whose names alone evoke true virtue. Some of Chrétien's figures are historically-identifiable knights, such as the King of Ireland's son or the King of Aragon, but the heroes of his works are the legendary figures. Considering that the figures in the *romans* by Chrétien are affiliated with the Arthurian realm, naturally, several characters appear in storylines in which they are not the primary subject. That is to say that, Lancelot plays a part in the tournament in the romance *Cligés*, but is also the central male character of *La Charrete*. The knight Sagremors, appears in *Cligés* as well as in *Erec et Enide*. Gawain participates in each tournament in *Erec et Enide*, *La Charrete*, *Perceval* and *Cligés*.

Unlike Chrétien's characters, the knights in the biographical narrative are just about all historical men whose existence can be proven and whose signatures appear on documents, e.g., William himself as a witness to the 1215 Magna Carta ("nobilium virorum Willielmi Marescalli Comitis Pembrochiæ.")[7] And the following historical figures show up repeatedly in *Le Maréchal*: Philippe, the Count of Flanders appears in five tournaments; the young king Henry of England appears in seven, and of course, William appears in all sixteen. In addition to William and the above named men, there are around eight others who are identified on a regular basis, including, Renaut de Nevers, the Count of Clermont, and the Count of Boulogne. On occasion, suffering from a convenient memory lapse, the narrator says he will not give any other names except William Marshal's because he does not remember them ("E s'aucuns des autres i olt, / Ge n'ai pas les nons en memorie" [vv. 4326–4327]). He does, however, find an incredible number of names in his memory for the tournament at Lagni sur Marne. It obviously is such an important competition that the author lists, by name and/or title, over ninety knights in a passage totaling 268 verses (vv. 4481–4749).

The names of the participants in the biographical narrative, perhaps not surprisingly, reflect the era.[8] The names of Guillaume, Henri, Robert and Baudouin are a few among the common ones found in the biographical narrative. This point is made because, in the fictional works, none of the heroes or central characters bears such an ordinary name. Their more unusual names, such as Ipomedon, Amadas and Perceval, are less representative of a particular time than other aforementioned ones. They were selected by the author of a fictional work with, no doubt, a specific symbolism[9] in mind, which adds to the legendary atmosphere and mystery that surround such characters.

In contrast to the high ideals embodied by such knights as Lancelot and Gawain, there are others, less well-known, whose names can conjure up negative qualities. In *Erec et Enide*, during the tournament, the "Proud One of the Moor" ("Li Orguelleus de la Lande" [v. 2137]) comes forth to joust with Erec. The adjective *orguelleus* is not necessarily derogatory, but it does denote a haughty, less than illustrious, attitude (Erec by the way, defeats him in a contest that may have symbolic significance). Elsewhere, in the same event, there is an unruly, "disorderly," knight ("Sagremors li Desreez" [v. 2193]), who despite his volatile profile and name, actually is a knight of great renown ("uns chevaliers de molt grant pris" [v. 2202]). In *Ipomedon*, there also appears the adjective "unruly" to describe a knight: "Sicanius le desreié" (v. 6089); in *La Charrete*, a certain covetous knight is recognized ("Ignaures li covoitiez" [v. 5788]). In *Partonopeus de Blois*, one of the participants, Armans, is first identified as a "Sarasin," which in itself has negative connotations to followers of Christianity. He is further described as being physically unattractive and not a nice man: "Fors et fornis, lais et hisdos, / cruels et fel et mal artos" (vv. 8104–8105).[10]

The author, Hue de Rotelande goes into rich detail in *Ipomedon* when profiling and naming participants. He mentions not only which knights participate, but how much they do enjoy tourneying, how talented they are, and the number of men who accompany each of the named knights. Monesteüs, the son of the King of Ireland, is accompanied by one hundred of his brave men; Nestor, the Duke of Normandy, has sixty men with him; the Count of Brittany is there with fifty valiant men. In all, there are more than 1400 participants and Rotelande provides concentrated, complete profiles of many of them.

The number of participants in *Ipomedon* just mentioned, brings up the question of just how large were tournaments. The impressive numbers found in *Ipomedon* are, most likely, unusual for the average tournament, but certainly possible. This is supported by *Le Maréchal* where, even though inconsistent and on occasion vague, the author suggests a wide range of numbers throughout his accounts, all the way from 9 to over 3000. In about half of the tournaments, no precise total is given and he prefers to speak of certain *chevaliers* whom he names, but gives no other numbers, or he says there were "many" but that is all; in Tournament 6, in fact, there were so many knights that the whole countryside resembled ants: "toz li païs en formie" (v. 2929). In the remaining tournaments he leans towards more precision by saying there are "X" number of knights, but sometimes his figures denote the total number of men under one banner, othertimes they are comprehensive totals for the entire contest. For example, at Lagni sur Marne, there are at least 3000 knights present: "plus de trei(s) mile ou a tant" (v. 4782). The field is so filled with men that one cannot even see the ground ("Tote en formïout la campaingne, / Si esteit emplie la plaingne / Que de plaingne n'i aveit point" [vv. 4793–4795]).

Vast numbers of participants also are listed on occasion in the other sources; in *Amadas et Ydoine*, there are more than one hundred knights on their way to a tournament ("plus de cent" [v. 851]). The author of *Partonopeus de Blois* evokes a rather large figure because the knights arrive "Par cens, par deux cens, par milliers" (v. 7890). There is no final total for this particular tournament, however, another indication of the large number of participants in this one is that there are seven judges necessary to choose the victor. In *La Charrete*, Chrétien de Troyes playfully enumerates the numbers by composing a series of verses that sounds like a nursery rhyme:

> Chevalier vienent dis et dis,
> et vint et vint, et trante et trante,
> ça quatre vint et ça nonante,
> ça cent, ça plus et ça deus tanz. (vv. 5590–5593)

These add to over four hundred and suggest that the tournament is quite an important one, but rather than imparting a serious nature, Chrétien looks at the figures with a musical tone, much like the cadence of soldiers marching.

In all fairness to the stories where impressive quantities of participants are recorded and seem unbelievable, one must take into account the contemporaneous perception of numbers and accuracy because it varies so from the modern perception. The twelfth-century writers would not necessarily be concerned with the validity of their numerical figures, since such precision was not a consideration of the day.[11]

Seen in this light, it is understandable that authors may have inflated the numbers a bit. But owing to the popularity of the sport and the open areas where the early tournaments were held, there is a good chance that the large figures were not as incorrect as one might believe.

While scores of knights are recognized by name, there is a great deal of diversity in how each author treats the very topic. In *Amadas et Ydoine*, the only participant named during a tournament is the hero, Amadas. The author speaks vaguely of "knights" or of a "sire," and once he says Amadas defeated the brother of the King of France, but that is the extent of identification. In "Chaitivel," Marie de France does not name any of the participants, even though she says there are "deus milliers." In the *lai* "Doon," the father is named (hence the title), the son is not. In *Cligés*, Chrétien tries for a bit to be vague about the participants, speaking in general terms of the "baron de pris" and "li plus de la chevalerie" (v. 4587). He provides a reason though when he emphatically states that he will not delay the story by listing the various participants:

Cuidiez vos or que je vos die
Por feire demorer mon conte:
"Cil roi i furent, et cil conte,
Et cil, et cil, et cil i furent? (vv. 4588–4591)

But try as he might, he finds it impossible to ignore several of the participants; surely, in part, because each one is already considered a superior knight and his participation adds luster to the event. Even though Chrétien avoids long discourses on the knights he eventually names, he does plausibly integrate them into the account. He manages this by having each one he names joust with Cligés in the four-day time-frame. Belonging to King Arthur's team, Chrétien identifies "Sagremors li desreez," "Lanceloz del Lac," "Percevax li Galois" and "Gauvains." Ultimately, it is important that the identities of Cligés' opponents be known in order to show how extraordinary this hero's talents are. The fact that Cligés can defeat or equal them develops his character and enhances his reputation.[12] Based on the examples, whether a knight was identified by name or not is clearly subjective, and the authors took full advantage of this personal preference.

Participants in tournaments had to carefully weigh their decision to compete or not since tourneying was not favorably regarded by all governing bodies; most seriously, the Catholic Church condemned competitors as sinners. The debate over whether all knights were sinners because they competed in this sport not sanctioned by the Catholic Church has been around for centuries—surely since the first edicts against tourneying were issued. Critics base their arguments in the notion that the sport was an unholy exercise, and also in that it encouraged knights to sin.[13] Is this the same perception given by the literary sources? Of course, the sources will be biased in favor of their subjects and heroes, however, in all fairness to chivalry, the sport and its concept would not have survived for so long if every single knight practiced the seven sins and were truly a malicious sinner. In the narratives, there are several different portraits of characters, some are viewed unfavorably and even appear to sin; however these portraits tend to show the diversity of human nature itself rather than preach that the sport has twisted the men.

In the tale of Milun, Marie de France does allude to the capital sins of violence, jealousy and cruelty in the case of the father. She says that Milun is willing and ready to cross the sea quickly in order to damage another well-known knight's reputation, as well as inflict corporal harm on him ("Hastivement mer passera, / Si justera al chevalier / Pur lui leidir e empeirier" ["Milun," vv. 350–352]). His only reason for dislike of the opponent whom he has never met is the fellow's good reputation as a knight ("Mut ert dolenz, mut se pleigneit / Del chevalier ki tant valeit" ["Milun," vv. 343–344]). This is certainly an unbecoming trait because knights were to be courteous and humane towards their fellow man, including their opponents, and truly, the notion of such a sin suggested here is unsettling. But before one condemns Milun, his desires never come to fruition and his jealousy is more of a confidence-builder than a true evil trait. Milun is basically a good person and does not carry out his initial threat even on the playing field. In such a light, he can be forgiven his unbecoming and briefly-lived attitude.

In *Amadas et Ydoine*, a few nobles are spoken of rather disdainfully for their participation in a tournament. First, the author ridicules the participation of the brother to the King of France as an act of pride and arrogance:

Freres estoit le roi de France,
Par grant orguel et par beubance
Avoit pris, et par aatie,
Un tournoi, et par grant envie. (vv. 1521–1524)

It is not just with one word but four that the baron is ridiculed. Two words are unmodified, "beubance"[14] and "aatie," and two augmented by an adjective, "grant orguel" and "grant envie." Further in the story, two barons wish to hold a tournament, not for pleasure but through pride (*par fierté*) and haughtiness (*par orgueil*).[15] These traits of pride and arrogance are unmistakable, but each of these persons is characterized by these sins well before the tournament itself. They may very well be sinners, but it is not because of the tournament, and whatever negative attributes they possess manifested themselves before the tournament. On the whole, the representation of knights' conduct in or around the tournament is not portrayed as sinful in and of itself, and this is more likely the norm rather than a rarity.

Overwhelmingly, the men who take part in tourneying are depicted as good men, the greatest, most valiant, they enjoy the highest of reputations, and are of good heart with few, if any, disreputable qualities. Without exception to the literary genre, the authors were quick to point out the positive attributes. The most expert, boldest, and most handsome knights are on their way to competition in *Amadas et Ydoine* ("Bien bouhourdant et preu et bel" [v. 853]). In *Le Maréchal*, many times the elite and best men found anywhere compete (e.g. "Quer i furent tuit [a] eslite / Li meillor qui fus[s]ent trové / E qui meilz erent esprové" [vv. 3902–3904]). The participants in *Ipomedon* are also great knights ("grant chevalerie" [v. 3134]). The medallion of knighthood carried with it certain lifestyles, and, in general, the men who were knights lived up to the high standards expected of them.

Most assuredly, individual knights are singled out for their fine attributes; William Marshal is constantly referred to as a knight who leads an exemplary life ("mena si trés bele vie" [*Le Maréchal*, v. 1513]). He is admired in the tournaments for his incredible abilities: "Si le fist si outréement / Que tot le munde se merveille / de la force & de la merve[i] lle" (vv. 1490–1492). In fact, he is so admired that all knights wish to be like him, as his author frequently states:

Li Mareschals, qui d'autre terre
Ert la venuz por son pris quere,
I fist tant d'armes, c'est la some,
Qu'el tornei[e]ment n'out halt home,
Conte, baron ne bacheler,
Qui d'armes nel volsist sembler. (vv. 2997–3002)

William is the penultimate knight, and his loyalty is ever admired by his peers ("Si cuit que vos n'eüstes unkes / nul bacheler plus seit sanz gile" [vv. 1476–1477]). Praise of William's extraordinary persona continues throughout the narrative, yet this work is not unique in its zealous illumination of the exceptional qualities of its hero or other knights. The same virtues, such as prowess in tourneying, valor, and honesty to name a few, are noted time and time again for members of the chivalric orders. In "Chaitivel" Marie refers to the lovers' athleticism and notes that they all four tourney very well ("Si quatre dru bien le feseient" [v. 115]). During the tournament in *Erec et Enide*, the King of the Red City is described as very valiant and bold ("le roi de La Roge Cité, / qui molt estoit vaillanz et preuz" [vv. 2154–2155]). Randuraz, in the same story, is a knight of great prowess ("chevaliers ert de grant proesce" [v. 2147]). The Duke Antenor in *Ipomedon* is portrayed as very bold, stalwart, and proud, even in the midst of the action: "Li dux Antenor ert mut pruz / e mut hardiz e mut estuz" (vv. 3651–3652). Amadas is characterized as valiant and bold ("Et il est tant vaillans et prous" [*Amadas et Ydoine*, v. 4444]). The young boy in "Doon" wins each competition he enters ("N'i ot un seul tant i jostast / ne de sa main tant gaaingnast" [vv. 219–220]). The list of examples could continue, but it is unnecessary since it is clear that reiteration of chivalric traits of the competitors is a vital feature of the narratives.

Many knights became quite wealthy thanks to the tournament and its available acquisitions.[16] At the same time, these knights were generous with their wealth, distributing it among the less fortunate. Marie de France refers to this tendency in two lines in the *lai* "Le Laüstic" (vv. 21–22), where she suggests that there is great wealth to be acquired, spent (*despendeit*), or given away (*donot*) generously as a result of tourneying. Horses were one of the more valuable acquisitions, yet, in the tournament at Joigni, William Marshal gives one away after capturing it, merely because a young herald had asked him for one before the contest began. Indeed, William gives away much of what he wins at this particular tournament:

> E de gaaing rout il sa part;
> Mais molt largement le depart
> E as croisiez e as prisons,
> E molt quita de lor prisons
> Des cheval[i]ers qu'il aveit pris. (*Le Maréchal*, vv. 3557–3561)

Even when he acquires large quantities of riches, William gives away a great deal ("Mais souvent s'en reveneit riches; / & il n'ert pas avérs ne chiches / de despendre ce ku'il aveit" [vv. 1895–1897]). Generosity or *largesse*, was essential for a knight to maintain a good reputation, obviously, William enjoyed this virtue.

The hero of the biography is not alone in showering others with gifts or riches, and even when knights were no longer competing they still continued to possess a certain *largesse*; for example, despite the attention Erec gives his new wife, and even though Erec has essentially retired from the sport, he remains as good as ever in helping others:

> Molt petit de li s'esloignoit,
> mes ainz por ce moins ne donoit
> de rien nule a ses chevaliers,
> armes ne robes ne deniers.
> Nul leu n'avoit tornoiemant
> nes anveast, molt richemant
> apareilliez et atornez.
> Destriers lor donoit sejornez
> por tornoier et por joster,
> que qu'il li deüssent coster. (*Erec et Enide*, vv. 2411–2420)

Even as he takes leave of his father and is about to trek out on subsequent adventures, he makes sure his father will continue to provide his knight companions with any and all equipment that chivalry requires. Such a virtue does not come without criticism and there are many scholars[17] who believe the *largesse* displayed by a William or an Erec stems more from obligation rather than goodwill and unselfishness. Surely there existed knights who spent money out of guilt hoping to absolve themselves of sins or to buy political allies, but on the whole, literary representations reveal a sincere generosity on the part of the *chevaliers*. It appears more a natural aspect, truly an unquestioned one, of chivalry, and it proves to be one of the more enduring.

To many knights, tournaments were a means of livelihood, it was certainly a steady "profession" for William Marshal for at least a ten-year period and appears to be his only source of income during this decade.[18] But aside from this practical reason, knights were drawn to participate for numerous other reasons, some more purely ethical such as the defense of the honor of a *pucelle*, e.g., Gawain in *Perceval*. He initially has no intention of entering the tournament ("ne s'est del tornoi antremis" [v. 5072]), but does so for the sake of a young girl. In this regard, the young girl had been slapped in public by her sister, and Gawain is then persuaded to tourney on behalf of the youngster. He does compete so admirably he is able to win honor for the *pucelle* for whom he undertook the event.

There are several additional reasons for competing. In their own stories, Ipomedon and Partonopeus de Blois, compete in order to win the prize; in *Amadas et Ydoine*, two feuding barons schedule a tournament, no doubt to resolve political tensions. Love is the motivation for the four main participants to compete in "Chaitivel;" family tradition, as well as the search for acclaim, is the reason Cligés competes in his narrative. In the beginning of his story, Cligés' father, Alexander, passes his own images of knighthood on to his son. In fact, it is Alexander who beseeches his son to go to the court of King Arthur and test himself against the Bretons and French:

> Biax filz Cligés, ja ne savras
> Conuistre con bien tu vaudras
> De proesce ne de vertu,
> Se a la cort le roi Artu
> Ne te vas esprover einçois
> Et as Bretons et as Einglois. (vv. 2565–2570)

The son's life is to parallel that of his father's, and these early passages, although tangential to the tournament which occurs later, show the family similarities and traditions being carried on. In the *lais* "Milun" and "Doon," the same is true with the idea, inherent in the story, of the son following in the father's footsteps. The family tradition carried on by the sons in these *lais* is more striking than in *Cligés* because it is done so fortuitously. Neither son grows up under the tutelage of his biological father, thus neither is paternally influenced towards tourneying. The boys' choice of livelihood comes naturally.[19] The father and son in "Milun" are even more similar because they have reputations as the best two knights in the tournament where they meet as adversaries. The author says that Milun does very well and he is much praised: "Mut le fist bien en cel estur / E mut i fu preisiez le jur" (vv. 403–404). As for the son, no one can equal him: "Sur tuz les autres ot le cri; / Ne si pot nuls acumparer" (vv. 406–407). Of course, the two best knights must eventually confront one another in order to decide the ultimate victor; as the verse 407 notes, the younger one does win.

With all the reasons to compete in a tournament, though, the vast majority of knights competed primarily for their own reputations.[20] The author of *Le Maréchal* repeatedly says that William gains honor through the sport: e.g., "Qui onor conquert e gaainne" (v. 3012). William acquires fame and glory for himself, as well as enhances the reputation of those who ride with him. In "Le Laüstic," there is not a particular tournament described, but Marie de France alludes to the sport of tourneying in order to stress how the fine reputation of one young fellow (*bachelers*) has been enhanced by and is associated with the sport:

> Li autres fu un bachelers
> Bien coneüz entre ses pers,
> De pruësce, de grant valur,
> E volentiers feseit honur;
> Mut turneot e despendeit
> E bien donot ceo qu'il aveit. (vv. 17–22)

The favorable qualities of "pruësce," "valur," and "honur" are acquired by tourneying well and practicing the ethical codes of chivalry.

To achieve the most revered reputation, participation in as many tournaments as possible was crucial since it enabled a knight to show he was consistently good. Success in just one tournament was not enough exposure to acquire a dominant reputation, as is seen with Lancelot. In the tournament, for a time Lancelot does exceedingly well, but as soon as he begins to perform poorly, the other knights attribute his early success to a fluke. They believe that the first tournament undertaken by a novice (which they take him to be), gives him such strength—nowadays one would say adrenaline—that he is temporarily invincible:

> Espoir por ce si bien le fist
> Que mes d'armes ne s'antremist.
> Se fu si forz a son venir
> Qu'a lui ne se pooit tenir
> Nus chevaliers, tant fust senez,
> Qu'il feroit come forsenez. (*La Charrete*, vv. 5689–5694)

They believe that his talent is fleeting, and that it can only be proven via many victorious tournaments. In *Amadas et Ydoine*, proving himself in many tournaments is precisely what Amadas does when he travels very far and makes a name for himself. It is thanks to an abundance of tournaments that he has the chance to prove himself: e.g., "En Vimeu en Ponthieu, grant pose / Tournoie et par armes s'alose" (vv. 1381–1382). William Marshal and the Young King spend an entire year doing nothing except biding their time in *plaids*,[21] hunting, or at tournaments ("Près d'un an, qu'il ne s'atornérent / A nul[e] rien for[s] a pleidier / ou a bois ou a torn[e]ier" [*Le Maréchal*, vv. 2392–2394]). After this particular year, William spends another two years tourneying with another friend. As has been documented, William has an excellent renown for tourneying, acquired in part by his many years of experience.

Another feature of the participants in a tournament is their regional or if possible, national, affliliation. In "Milun" and "Chaitivel," although the knights themselves remain unnamed (except for Milun), their native territories are identified ("Normein e Bretun i alerent, / E li Flamenc e li Franceis" ["Milun," vv. 386–387], and "E li Franceis e li Norman / E li Flamenc e li Breban; / Li Buluineis, li Angevin" ["Chaitivel," vv. 77–79]). William Marshal and the Young King are often matched against knights from the continent ("De l'autre part furent Franceis, / Borgoignon, Flamenc, Hanoeis" [Le Maréchal, vv. 3211–3212]). The tournament at Lagni sur Marne, with its vast number of competitors, has a most extensive list of regional and national affiliations, which along with the aforementioned, includes "Engleis," "Angevin," Tieis,"[22] and "cels d'Avalterre."[23]

Considering the subject matter for the romans of Chrétien de Troyes, it is understandable that the knights found therein are generally from Britain, but he rarely makes note of their more specific homelands. In the other romances, Amadas is French, hailing from Burgundy, and Ipomedon is from the Kingdom of La Pouille.[24] In reviewing this aspect of the sources, it comes to light that the just mentioned romances do not stress the nationalities of the participants hence their origins are briefly noted. They place more emphasis on the individual knight and less on his native land. This is quite unlike the lais of Marie de France and the narrative of William Marshal where there is rather a lot of consistent emphasis on naming the homelands. Certainly, the "Normanz," "Franceis" and "Engleis" appear frequently. The romance Partonopeus de Blois does not favor any one land or domain, but it does identify the homeland affiliation almost each time a knight is discussed. To wit, there are kings of Syria, Persia, and France, as well as Brittany, Galice, Valence, and Navarre. There are emperors of Germany and Spain, and knights who are "Normans," "Britons," "Tiois," "Grifons," "Romans," "Frison," and even "Sarasin." Through these diverse lands, we can recognize the geographic expanse of the tournament's popularity; it was practiced by Christians as well as "Pagans."

The notion of tourneying's popularity among diametrically opposed religious factions warrants a brief discourse on the literary representation of the religious element, particularly since it is conspicuously absent from just about every source. In fact, in only one work are any knights affiliated with a religion, and this when they are being listed as participants in the tournament. Religious affiliations are mentioned in *Partonopeus de Blois* where they are nebulously classified as "Christians" and "Pagans." The majority of "Pagans" hailing from the Moorish territory, the rest from Arabia. And yet, having made the religious distinctions at the beginning of the event, the remainder of the tournament is devoid of religious themes, overtones, and these very same divisions. This is managed first, by not having the two teams conveniently divided into said religious groups, and secondly, by no longer mentioning the subject. Elsewhere in the works the knights may be portrayed as religious and devout. They may act as champions of the Catholic Church in crusades or be on a quest for Christianity, however, when the tournament approaches, the religious elements are not overtly noted. The absence of the religious aspect is not a complete surprise considering the Catholic Church's negative attitude towards tourneying, but it should be recognized as a cognizant choice made by the authors, and a choice not lightly made.

Before concluding this chapter, there is a knight who should be mentioned because he makes a personal choice which affects his chivalric life. The knight in question is Erec from *Erec et Enide*. His case is problematic because after his marriage to Enide, he chooses no longer to compete in tournaments and this deviates from the norms of chivalry. Erec is, in essence, rejecting the duties[25] expected of him by the elite society of which he is a member. Failing to live up to the expectations of the society places it and what it represents in danger and threatens its very existence.[26] Erec, in his choice to quit tourneying, disrupts the order and nature of what characterizes the chivalric realm— the tournament. As long as Erec competes, he is the boldest, most loyal and most courteous knight in the land ("li plus hardiz et li plus fiers / li plus leax, li plus cortois" [vv. 2462–2463]). Once he stops competing, however, his reputation suffers greatly, as his wife points out:

> Vostre pris est molt abessiez:
> tuit soloient dire l'autre an
> qu'an tot le mont ne savoit l'an
> meillor chevalier ne plus preu;
> Vostres parauz n'estoit nul leu.
> Or se vont tuit de vos gabant,
> juesne et chenu, petit et grant;
> recreant vos apelent tuit. (vv. 2510–2517)

Because he forsakes the tournament and its ideals, Erec is disgraced and is cruelly ridiculed by the folk. His public lack of ambition and his absence are a source of concern to his companions, but are necessary for the narrative since his subsequent adventures are an indirect result of said decision.

One feature not dealt with is whether or not knights are officially dubbed. While it was more likely that a man was already dubbed a knight when competing, there are cases of men who are not dubbed as knights competing in tournaments.[27] For those men in these sources, however, all are officially recognized as knights and the question is not broached. Since the ceremony has little pertinence to the tournament itself and should occur before a contest, there is no reason to mention it or whether a competitor has official status as a knight, thus this aspect is absent in the tournament accounts themselves.

It is understandable and natural to read an account of a tournament and regard each competitor as a one-dimensional knightly figure. However, through the various examples provided, it is clear that underneath the auspices of knighthood, all kinds of individuals were represented in the literary tournament. Each second or third "label" attached to a knight not only adds another dimension to his persona but also helps make each tournament distinctive.

Notes

1. The exception being Gawain; see chapter on heraldry.

2. The verse referring to this knowledge is problematic, "Li uns de l'autre le saveit" (v. 59). It is in constant dispute by scholars because it actually says the knights *did* know of each other; however, there must be an error in the manuscript because the rest of the story would not make sense if they did know each other, and were aware of the lady's love for each.

3. "Les rois, de plus, avaient grand'peine à se priver eux-mêmes de ces jeux; ils oubliaient souvent leurs propres ordonnances et donnaient l'exemple de les enfreindre." Jusserand, 304–05.

4. They may be "mere" knights, but they do acquire their own level of importance. In a passage in *Amadas et Ydoine*, a young boy, believing Amadas to be just a bourgeois, passes Amadas at first without noticing him (or ignores him). Once the boy discovers Amadas is a knight ("Bien voit que il n'est pas borjois / Ains set bien qu'il est chevaliers" [vv. 4072–4073]) he can tell Amadas his mission. Such an encounter implies that knights are privy to certain information not afforded to others.

5. *Le Maréchal*, vv. 2627–2630.

6. It is not my intent to provoke arguments concerning the legendary or historical status of these characters, but owing to the lack of any concrete evidence of the existence of the Knights of the Round Table, I will treat them as legend.

7. Thomson, 64.

8. This is an observation substantiated by Michel Pastoureau: "Les deux noms d'hommes les plus répandus sont les mêmes en France et en Angleterre: Jean et Guillaume. Ensuite on rencontre, en Angleterre: Robert, Richard, Thomas, Geoffroy, Hugues et Etienne; en France: Pierre, Philippe, Henri, Robert et Charles. La vogue de certaines autres est plus particulière à une province: Baudouin en Flandres, Thibaud en Champagne." Pastoureau, 16.

9. "La symbolique du nom, et singulièrement du nom propre, apparaît en définitive très présente, très vivante, dans les œuvres médiévales. Héritière à cet égard d'une tradition fort ancienne, la civilisation du Moyen Age y a trouvé de surcroît l'occasion de dépasser l'anecdotique pour atteindre à l'exemplaire. Le nom, qu'il soit générique ou individualisé, est toujours porteur d'un message qu'il faut s'efforcer d'interpréter, de "décoder"—et il confère au personnage qui le porte ou à l'œuvre qu'il désigne une valeur typifiante qui en assure la pérennité." Ribard, 89–90.

10. According to the glossary in the work, *fel* means "perfide or déloyal." In the *Larousse Dictionary of the Moyen Age*, *hisdos* is defined as an adjective

from unknown Germanic origins meaning "frightening, horrible." (p. 311). In Larousse, *mal artos* is defined as "malhonnête" (p. 40).

11.   "The truth is that the regard for accuracy, with its firmest buttress, the respect for figures, remained profoundly alien to the minds even of the leading men of that age." Bloch, *Feudal Society*, 75.

12.   "Se mesurer dans un tournoi aux compagnons de la Table Ronde est le meilleur moyen de consacrer sa valeur, mais la véritable critère est un combat contre Gauvain. . . ." Marie-Luce Chênerie, "Ces curieux chevaliers tournoyeurs . . ." des fabliaux aux romans" *Romania* 97 no. 3 (1976): 327–68; 343.

13.   "Il faut bien donner raison à Jacques de Vitry, les tournois multipliaient les occasions de commettre les sept péchés captitaux. Les conduites vaniteuses, les convoitises, les désordres sociaux, l'engrenage des folles dépenses et de l'usure, la violence, la cruauté, . . . Chênerie," "Ces Curieux," 347.

14.   In the glossary definition from *Aiol*, *beubant* is defined as *arrogance*. Jacques Normand and Gaston Raynaud, eds., *Aiol* (Paris: Libraries de Firmin Didot et Cie, 1877), 326.

15.   These are the modern French translations made by the editor. Aubailly, 37.

16.   See chapter on winnings for a more complete discussion.

17.   "Pour les riches, le tournoi est l'occasion de dépenser, de gaspiller, comme par une obligation de classe." Chênerie, "Ces Curieux . . . ," 331. As discussed in another chapter, tournaments did become lavish and pompous affairs in later centuries. At such time, it was an extravagant event where wealth was distributed in order to show off, and there was little sincere *largesse*. But to say all knights, certainly those in the early days of the sport, spent money out of obligation, or wasted money, is a bit harsh and many do not warrant such criticism.

18.   "Les tournois étaient, en effet, par les prises qu'on y pouvait faire, un moyen de gagner ou de perdre de l'argent. Certains chevaliers en vivaient, et Guillaume le Maréchal fut certainement, pendant sa jeunesse, l'un de ceux-là." Meyer, *Le Maréchal*, vol. 3, intro. p. xxxix.

19.   This is a notion which can go so far as to suggest chivalric talents can be inherited through some sort of familial bond, however, chances are the reasons are less mystic, and are more likely because the sport was popular and most young boys grew up dreaming of becoming a knight. Naturally, they would learn how to tourney and choose this lifestyle over more mundane ones.

20.   Such a remark could of course lead a critic to argue that knights were selfish. However, one must consider that knights, in many ways, were "doing their job," "making a living," and it was important to take an interest in and be concerned about one's public perception. The same holds true today because people strive to take pride in their work. What is difficult to recognize is that

tourneying was the way of life for those who had become knights and the concept of earning one's income or whatever came with victory, was not necessarily contested or frowned upon.

21.   According to Paul Meyer's glossary, *plaids* are a type of joust with different rules from those in a tournament. A *plaid* is also considered less honorable than a tournament. See *Le Maréchal*, vol. 2, p. 374.

22.   ". . . mais ici les Tiois, étant mentionnés à côté des Flamands et de "ceux d'Avalterre," ne peuvent être que des Allemands." Meyer, *Le Maréchal*, vol. 3 (footnote), 51.

23.   This refers to men from the Low Countries and further east, extending all the way to Cologne. See Meyer, *Le Maréchal,* vol. 3 (footnote), 51.

24.   La Pouille is the modern day region of Apulia, in southeastern Italy. It is now governed by the Italian government but was under Norman domination in the eleventh and twelfth centuries. The kingdom acquired an Italian born king (Frederic II) in 1197.

25.   "Erec a oublié les devoirs de chevalerie entre les bras d'Enide." LeGoff, 196.

26.   ". . . l'ordre est mis en danger par ceux de ses membres qui oublieraient leur devoir." Köhler, 30.

27.   "Moreover, there are several early examples of non-knights tourneying." Barker, *The Tournament*, 115. Ms. Barker then goes into further detail of who some of these knights were.

Chapter VI

Heraldry

Heraldry, with its colors and symbols, is understood to encompass: shields, coats of arms, banners, and crests. Its existence was crucial for recognition of one's teammates, and enhanced the bonds of fraternity amongst knights which prevailed at a tournament. Noticeably, though, much like the heralds themselves who rarely appear in the early works, heraldry too, plays only a sporadic role in the works of the day. On the occasions it does play a role though, heraldry is an important, interesting, and decisive feature.

Heraldry did not evolve out of the tournament, rather, the tournament adopted it as a visual means of communication. The existence of shields and pennants with emblems sewn or carved on them is seen early in the Middle Ages, prior to any evidence of tourneying.[1] The well-known *Tapisserie de Bayeux* (circa 1080) is an excellent visual example of early heraldic aspects. Knights are therein depicted carrying pennants that have a certain insignia, or shields with fantastic animals. The tapestry shows numerous variations of crosses and apparent dragons.[2] The colors include shades of red, green, and blue; there are shields with dots, while others are completely unadorned. Under each respective insignia a unit bands together for war, just as units will later band together in tournaments. Since the 'art of blazoning'[3] was a known practice of *seigneurs* and the likes well before tourneying is mentioned in literature, the minimalization, as seen in the literature, of its use in the early days of the sport is notable, and because the authors who take care to detail and speak of shields and crests are relatively few, any attention given to heraldry must be of significance to their story.

Chrétien de Troyes is one of those authors and his *La Charrete* is perhaps the earliest work in the sources to deal with heraldry and its iconography. In this *roman*, Lancelot is imprisoned just before the

great tournament is to begin; he obtains permission to leave his prison
for the purpose of participating, but alas, has no equipment. He is
allowed to use the arms and horse of his captor, lent to him, ironically
enough, by the mistress of his prison, wife of his captor ("Et la dame
tantost li baille / les armes son seignor, vermoilles, / et le cheval qui
a mervoilles" [vv. 5498–5500]). It is at this time that heraldry becomes a prominent feature of the story. Lancelot journeys on to the
town of Noauz where the tournament will be held. Greatly tired, he
undresses in an inn and places his shield outside the door of the
lodging. Shortly after, a herald-at-arms chances upon the shield. Since
the plain red shield does not really belong to Lancelot, it does not
have his personal crest; consequently, the herald cannot determine
the shield's owner:

> un hyraut d'armes, an chemise, . . .
> L'escu trova a l'uis devant,
> Si l'esgarda; mes ne pot estre
> qu'il coneüst lui ne son mestre;
> ne set qui porter le devoit. (vv. 5537–5545)

The *hyraut* can learn the identity of the knight only when he peeks
through the open door and spies Lancelot on the bed. In turn uncov-
ered by Lancelot, the herald is sworn to secrecy about Lancelot's true
identity. Because he has not been betrayed, no one, try as they might,
during the eventual tournament (apart from the Queen who has her
suspicions) is able to identify the shield and knight. Lancelot remains
unknown even to Gawain, who does not recognize him. Amazed at
the outstanding skills of the Red Knight, as Lancelot becomes known
("Li chevaliers vermauz"), Gawain is content merely to watch his performance:

> Gauvains d'armes ne se mesla
> qui ert avoec les autres la;
> qu'a esgarder tant li pleisoit
> les proesces que cil feisoit. (vv. 5953–5956)

Gawain is in fact searching for his friend Lancelot, but cannot find
him. It is amusing then, that Lancelot is able to fight for two days
directly in front of Gawain without being discovered.

In an almost tragic result, the fact that Lancelot is unrecognizable
also proves to be quite dangerous. At one point during the chaos on
the field, the Queen suspects that the mysterious knight is the man of

her heart although she cannot identify the shield he uses; so she sends instructions to him. Should the Red Knight obey the instructions, the Queen's suspicions will be confirmed, and they are. However, in obeying the instructions, Lancelot endures many severe blows and certainly runs the risk of being killed. It is ultimately, then, the faithfulness of the Red Knight, not his armor, which allows the Queen to identify him. The heraldry proves to be an important factor during the tournament because it allows Lancelot to participate surreptitiously and in doing so, prove his devotion.

Partonopeus de Blois is in a similar predicament to Lancelot's inasmuch as he too, is being held captive shortly before the tournament. Partonopeus also must borrow the armor of his jailkeeper, and like Lancelot, when he competes, he is not recognized by any heraldic traits. The author of this romance though, unlike Chrétien, keeps the descriptions of heraldry to a minimum, revealing only that Partonopeus' shield is silver and his horse handsome. The element of heraldry serves little in this scene except to render Partonopeus mysterious.

Cligés and Ipomedon in their own romances also compete in armor that no one recognizes, but they have willing chosen to do so. The different heraldry they acquire disguises each hero and provides them with multiple identities. At the end of each day, Cligés puts away his worn armor and places outside his door the unused armor he plans to wear the next day. The knights, thus befuddled, can determine neither his domicile nor his identity. Cligés' heraldry is an ally in his quest to be accepted as a valiant knight in his own right. Ipomedon also changes into different armor which he uses as a disguise; however, since he has been keeping many things hidden even before the tournament, his predilection for switching armor comes as little surprise to the reader.

In the romances, Chrétien de Troyes exploits heraldry, not only for thematic reasons of anonymity, as seen in *La Charrete*, but additionally for the visual effects it ables him to create in the text. He is one of the authors most devoted to heraldry and relies on it extensively. For example, the second day of Lancelot's tournament, knights who are not competing and are sitting in the stands describe the heraldry for those ladies present. Not content to describe just a few shields, the knights point out a large number of them to the ladies watching, taking pains all the while to identify the owners:

> et cil lor armes lor devisent
> des chevaliers que il plus prisent.
> Antr'ax dïent: "Veez vos or

celui a cele bande d'or
par mi cel escu de bernic?
C'est Governauz de Roberdic.
Et veez vos celui aprés
qui an son escu pres a pres
a mise une aigle et un dragon?
C'est li filz le roi d'Arragon. (vv. 5771–5780)

In addition to the above names, the knights further tell of Ignaures the Covetous and his half blue shield that has a leopard on a green background on the other half ("sor le vert point un liepart" [v. 5786]). They continue to note a shield with pheasants beak to beak (". . .les feisanz / an son escu poinz bec a bec" [vv. 5790–5791]); this particular shield belongs to Coguillanz of Mautirec. A knight named Semiramis has a shield with dark lions, themselves on gold shields ("as escuz d'or as lÿons bis" [v. 5795]). On King Yder's shield is a stag appearing to pass through a gate ("an son escu pointe une porte? / Si sanble qu'il s'an isse uns cer" [vv. 5800–5801]). Thoas the Young One, carries a shield with two swallows appearing to fly (". . .deus arondres / qui sanblent que voler s'an doivent" [vv. 5818–5819]). The knights proceed further and mention how the shields were made ("reçoivent / mainz cos des aciers poitevins" [vv. 5820–5821]), and whence they came ("de Lÿon sor le Rosne," "Londres," and "Tolose."). Precise information such as the far-away lands whence the shields hail help add to the splendor of the colorful descriptions.

The designs and emblems are remarkable for they are diverse and vividly described by Chrétien. He is meticulous with the choice of colors such as "or" and "bernic." *Bernic* (or *belic/belif*) is a rare word for a shade of red and ordinarily designates a type of insignia in that shade.[4] He employs "bernic" instead of a more standard word for red first and simply, in order to rhyme with the proper noun Roberdic, but nonetheless important is its evocation of a richer image. Chrétien is certainly aware of the visual possibilities available through heraldic descriptions, and clearly exploits them in lengthy portions in *La Charrete*; he devotes about forty-nine verses to the shields in one passage alone. The vibrant colors and images paint a pleasing picture which offsets to some extent the more chaotic aspects of the tournament. It is noteworthy that Chrétien says as much as he does about heraldry in this story, for, as William Kibler has pointed out, "The use here [in *La Charrete*] of personal and family devices for decoration and identification is remarkable, for this was not widespread until the thirteenth century."[5] What the details reveal is that heraldry was beginning to be well-noticed and more specific in design.

While *La Charrete* contains the most substantial recounting, it is not the only romance Chrétien replenishes with heraldic splendor; for example in *Cligés*, he takes time to mention assorted colors, fruits, and shields, although not to the same extent. He does note Lancelot's gold shield with a lion on it ("Sor l'escu d'or a lyon point" [v. 4741]), and mentions the colors of each of Cligés' four shields (black, green, red, and white). Chrétien compares Cligés' black armor to a mulberry fruit and finds the armor blacker ("Plus noire que more meüre / Noire fu s'armeüre tote" [vv. 4615–4616]), implying that anything related to worthy knights surpasses all others of its kind. But aside from a few other observations on color, this is the extent of the heraldry in *Cligés*.

In *Amadas et Ydoine*, the first detailed mention of an individual's heraldry at a tournament is made after Amadas is cured and is arriving at a tournament with his attendants. The author does not hesitate to describe the brilliant, glimmering lances adorned with silk cloth that floats in the wind: "Blance, flourie, a fer luisant / et a pignoncel ventelant / de blanc cendal, de soie fine" (vv. 4281–4283). Amadas himself has "Som blanc escu, qu'il ot couvert / de l'isembrun noir detrencié" (vv. 4290–4291). The contrast here of Amadas' white shield draped in a black cloth is as striking as Chrétien's contrast of dark lions on gold shields in *La Charrete*, and in being so, readily conveys a vivid image. The poet goes on to note that the helmet worn by Amadas is of gold ("Et ou hiaume qui a or fu" [v. 4404]), quite a grandiose feature since gold was an expensive element even in his day. The anticipation for the tournament is enhanced by the minute details of the armor because it reveals extra care taken for the upcoming event, certainly giving it credence as an important one. At an earlier stage on their way to tourney, knights are also described with enthusiasm: "Qu'en la route a mult biaus escus, / Haubers saffrés, hiaumes agus, / Riches chevaus et de grant pris" (vv. 1603–1605). The adjectives "saffrés," "biaus," and "agus" while partly a poetic trait of coloring, serve additionally to brighten an otherwise dull, and quickly told, picture of knights who were travelling along a road.

Occasionally Marie de France suggests that heraldry is crucial to a knight. In "Milun," at the tournament at Mont St. Michel, Milun's adversary is quickly identified by his trappings ("A ses armes, a ses escuz" [v. 394]) and, therefore, readily pointed out to Milun. Both Milun and his adversary are obviously ignorant of each other's heraldic personal

markings because the only way that Milun is able to identify the opponent as his son is later through a family ring ("Al dei celui cunuit l'anel"
[v. 430]), not through a particular shield and its emblems. Despite its
failure to identify the fellow to Milun, the heraldry was initially important to focus in on Milun's counterpart. In her tale of "Chaitivel," the
banners are what prove to be of interest. Before the tournament begins, the four primary knights carry the banner (*gumfanun*) or other
tokens of love ("Tuit portouent sa druërie, / Anel u mance u gumfanun"
[vv. 68–69]) of the lady who is sponsoring the event. They openly
carry these before the start of the game to show their devotion to her,
however, by the time the competition begins, her personal items are
replaced and each baron-knight carries his own banner (*enseignes*):
"Cil defors les unt coneüz / As enseignes e as escuz" (vv. 89–90), any
other tokens of the lady are not visible. At this point in the action,
each knight carries his own banner in order to be identified with a
team.[6] It is through their banners, as well as their shields, that they are
recognized in their own right at the tournament. Marie goes into no
further detail about emblems or design, and she does not use any
colors to illustrate the banners or shields of the knights, but the brevity of the *lais* helps to explain in part her superficial treatment of
heraldry. To refer to the anonymous *lai* "Doon," there is no mention
of heraldry or colors at all during the tournament and in turn, no
recognition between the central characters on the playing field ("Mes
il ne sot que il estoit, / Ne Doon ne le connoissoit" [vv. 231–231]). It
is not until the central characters begin to talk about the past and the
young boy shows Doon a ring, that they discover they are father and
son.

There are periodic glimpses of heraldry in *Partonopeus de Blois*,
but they are fleeting and weak. For example, when the queen remarks
that the knight with the silver shield is good, silver is the only specifi-
cation of the shield. Elsewhere, the Sultan of Persia is said to be hand-
somely and richly armed, but details go no further. The judges discuss
a knight who has a white shield ("li blaus escus"), and banners are
mentioned, yet nothing is visualized with colors or emblems. Besides
the two shields specified, one white and the other silver, there is no
elaboration on heraldry in the portion of the narrative that has survived.

The fictional works have shown precise combinations of emblem
and color when speaking of heraldry; curiously, the same cannot be
said for *Le Maréchal*. Juliet Barker observes that "William Marshal,
for instance, was recognized by the Count of St Pol across a tourna-

ment field because of the arms displayed on the shield."[7] While Barker is correct in her observation, she does not note that, although the shield has "arms displayed," none of these is described in the tournament text. In *Le Maréchal*, there exists the total absence of colors or emblems whenever a tournament is recounted. In just five tournaments does the biographer even allude nebulously to the banner (*baniére*) or standard of a team; to cite two examples: "Li giemble reis o sa baniére" (v. 5527), and "Quinze i out baniéres portant" (v. 4772). None of the other tournaments has the word *baniére*. Since the poet is quite capable of using adjectives, it is remarkable that no banner is identified by color, emblem, or any substantive marking. The absence of concise details on heraldry here is furthermore remarkable because the author mentions several times that banners and shields were recognized during the tournament; the problem is they are not described ("E sa baniére ert quenuüe / par tot la ou ele ert veüe [vv. 4659–4660], and "Dès qu'il out veü son escu / Quer de molt loing lout queneü" [vv. 5597–5598]). In Tournament 12, at Lagni sur Marne, the author writes seventeen times that a "banner" is being carried, but never once describes a single one. Another case in point is during Tournament 2. While this tournament is taking place, the Good Abbot of Rogi asks Johan de Soleingni to identify a particular knight, and he does, who, coincidently, happens to be William Marshal. In doing so, Johan says that William is carrying the shield of the Tancarville family: "sis escuz est de Tankarvile" (v. 1478). The proper noun Tancarville, with which William is affiliated, is the only identified mark of heraldic nature in this scene.

The examples show that heraldry was a prominent feature of the sport, yet, the author of *Le Maréchal* did not find it necessary for his story to pursue the various designs. He chose not to provide visual images of any pennants or shields present at the tournaments even though they clearly existed at the time. William Marshal even had his own heraldry which consisted of "Parted per pale Or and Vert, a Lion rampant Gules, armed and langued Azure; . . ."[8] As has been shown, it is well-known that shields and banners were typically decorated with figures and colors, yet by the total omission of these same heraldic features, the author most noticeably, has altered his subject matter. Such a choice shortens the biographical narrative, but one must wonder, to what avail? Perhaps it can be explained in terms of "frills or no frills," that is to say, to omit the finer details of the heraldry lends a more matter-of-fact tone to the scene. The author must consider it

inappropriate to expand on the "extraneous" features of a tournament. He concentrates instead on what is directly pertinent to his
subject, i.e., William Marshal. The opponents and teammates deserve
a mention in order to establish William's rank among them. His prowess and gains are important to show how successful he is. As will be
seen, the sights and sounds of the carnage are appropriate to show
how dangerous tourneying is so, in turn, when William leaves unscathed his reputation will be enhanced. The author refrains from
elaborating on heraldry, unlike Chrétien de Troyes, because descriptions of the sort do not belong in his biography inasmuch as they do
not develop or elevate the grandeur of his hero. In this regard, the
fictional works prove to be richer, and consequently, more accurate
with this highlighted aspect.

Whether heraldry itself is actually discussed or not in the sources,
the assortment of animals heretofore listed is interesting and warrants
a look because each animal is a powerful or independent creature. To
reiterate, there are: leopards, pheasants, lions, stags, swallows, eagles,
and dragons. Considering the poets made note of these particular
creatures (and while there are surely more), they also deserve a remark because they lend insight into the figures who chose and wore
them. The choice of a specific animal was generally linked in some
personal way with the knight; as Pastoureau has researched, the choice
could be merely a matter of taste, a designation of the family trade or
even symbolic, although this was not a term used contemporaneously.
Physical attributes could also be associated with an animal: "le lion
évoque la force, le mouton l'innocence, le sanglier le courage, la croix
le chrétien, etc."[9] Of particular interest is the dragon portrayed on the
shield of the King of Aragon's son (*La Charrete*, vv. 5779–5780). It
is a bit abrupt to see on a knight (who in essence is to be a representative of all that is good), the figure of the dragon since it is considered
a mythical creature whose origins are associated with evil; however,
its appearance is less surprising and better understood when the "evolution" of the dragon figure is briefly recounted.

The dragon appears early in literature in a narrative about Saint
Marcellus, Bishop of Paris, who defeats one; hence, an apparent battle
of good over evil. Such a metaphorical victory has been identified by
Jacques LeGoff who also sees the saint's victory over the dragon as
symbolic: "in its sixth-century literary form in Fortunatus' text, it [the
dragon] seems to be no more than one of those dragons which served
as attributes for a good many saints, particularly evangelical bishop-

saints, symbolizing the devil and paganism."[10] While taking into account the dragon's initial symbolism of evil, LeGoff recognizes that in later centuries it develops further into two divergent ideas; one where it becomes nothing more symbolic than a processional *mores*.[11] The other idea is that the dragon becomes symbolic for a non-secular group: "over the course of the twelfth century, however, the standard-dragon developed a symbolism of its own, the upshot of which was to make the dragon the emblem first of a military community, then of a nation."[12] This "military community" is most likely the chivalric realm, as evidenced by the dragon's portrayal on shields such as that of the Aragon prince. How fascinating for the dragon to progress from "evil" to "good" and experience an identity crisis inasmuch as what it first represented was lost during liturgical parades.[13] Although LeGoff illuminates the basis for the dragon, he does not find a hearty explanation for its depiction on knightly shields other than a religious one when knights were helping the "clergy in fighting the monster."[14] I should like to think that in the late-twelfth and early-thirteenth centuries, the knights felt the dragon represented a newly acquired persona of positive power and independence; surely in *La Charrete* it represents a strong and independent creature. Its appearance on a shield side by side with an eagle is evidence of a change in the mystique surrounding dragons, making it less evil, but all the same, formidable and powerful.

And while the symbolic significance of the colors of heraldry is not a primary focus, it is relevant to point out some of the more popular ones as they appear, and cases where the symbolism in each is implicit. The colors in question are red (*roge* or *vermoille*), black (*noir*), green (*verz* or *vert*), and white (*blan*). Red is a rich color;[15] the color *vermoille* is actually a brighter red (*rouge vif*).[16] In the Catholic liturgical world of colors, red is symbolic of martyrs and apostles. Is it hardly surprising then, that Lancelot wears red in the tournament in *La Charrete* since surely each definition of the color can apply to his appearance there. The red reflects the brightness and splendor of his true performance; it could also be said that Lancelot is almost a martyr because he is willing to obey the Queen no matter the cost—which is nearly his life. So Lancelot is the Red Knight, and in the end, much admired by all and as brilliant as his armor.

Black is a much different color than red, generally associated with the dark side, all that is unpleasant and ugly.[17] It is however, the first color Cligés chooses to wear. In partial explanation of the choices

Cligés makes in colors, according to Jacques Ribard, the four colors have little to do with Cligés' own personality, rather they correspond to each of the knights, and their associative terrestrial elements, he is to fight. Black, then, representing the earth, symbolizes the personality of Sagremors, Cligés' first opponent.[18] The next color chosen by Cligés is green, one of the more popular ones of the day, making him the Green Knight. Green is a color of light and clarity. According to Ott, green is a much more diverse color for symbolism because it stands for positive as well as negative attributes: "A l'idée de *vert* s'associe celle de la *croissance*, de la *prospérité*; on applique ce vocable de *vert* à tout ce qui est dans sa jeunesse, à tout ce qui vit d'une forte et jeune vie."[19] Green is the dominant color of nature and represents the lifecycle, ironically though, it is also a shade of bile and jealousy.[20] And despite the negative connotations associated with the color green such as jealousy, in *Cligés*, Ribard believes it to represent water, which then corresponds nicely to his opponent, Lancelot who is the Knight of the Lake. Cligés chooses *vermoille* the third day, and on the fourth day of the tournament at Osenefort, he chooses to wear the vestments in which he was knighted ("Et fet les armes aporter / Dom il fu noviax chevaliers" [vv. 4824–4825]); his shield is of ivory all else is white:

> Ne n'i ot color ne pointure:
> Tote fu blance s'armeüre,
> Et li destriers et li hernois
> Si fu plus blans que nule nois. (vv. 3987–3990)

The white Cligés wears on the last day is in total contrast with the black he wore on the first. White is a pleasing color, soothing and agreeable to human perceptions.[21] Cligés is aware that his identity will be revealed on the last day and the color white aids in his shining performance. It is the color of innocence and purity[22] and thus, represents Cligés' innocence and vulnerability in his first encounter with the great King Arthur. In addition, white is the "signe de perfection"[23] and corresponds to Gawain, the untainted knight, and the only opponent Cligés is unable to defeat. In fact, they spar so equally well that their match is stopped by King Arthur because he recognizes neither will dominate the other. In this tournament, Cligés reveals his pure state of being, and shows himself to be a reflection of Gawain.

In the romance *Ipomedon*, as in *Cligés*, there is a similar stark contrast of colors, but almost entirely in reverse. The first day of the tournament Ipomedon wears all white:

Od un blanc penuncel fermé
E blanche lance e blanc escu,
Sur un cheval set blanc kernu;
Il est tut blancs, cist chevalers. (vv. 3594–3597)

The repetition of color in these four lines is certainly reminiscent of
Cligés. For his last day, Ipomedon is in all black (*neir*):

Tut en meine sun neir herneis,
Sur neir destrer, sun neir escu
E sa lance, ke neire fu,
Ffet porter od l'enseigne neire. (vv. 5542–5545)

Elsewhere, in *Erec et Enide*, Chrétien devotes twenty-one lines (vv.
2100–2120) to the designs and colors of the banners and lances;
some painted "d'azur" and "sinople." Other lances are striped (*bandée*)
or variegated (*veire*). He speaks of helmets "de fer et d'acier," or others "vert," "giaune," and "vermoil." There are "blazon" and "hauberc
blanc," as well as shields with colors of azur or "d'argent a bocles
d'or." All popular colors and patterns of the age, and passages such
as these give much color to the literary event.

Clearly, Hue de Rotelande and Chrétien de Troyes provide the reader
with many colors because they add to the tournament's emerging the-
atrical atmosphere as well as create a dramatic visual effect. In this
regard, there is a marked difference between the fictional works and
the biographical narrative. Heraldry, barely mentioned in *Le Maréchal*,
is apparently not as necessary a factor in recounting the tournament
as it is to the romance writers who give it much fuller treatment. Heraldry, although not as stylish as it was to become in later centuries, is
an integral element of the tournament, and as such, is treated most
richly in the romance tradition.

Notes

1. "Heraldry, or the 'art of blazoning,' as a phasis of feudalism, dates from the tenth century, and is said to have been initiated by Henry Duke of Saxony, about A.D. 919." Bell, 97.

2. Dragons here represent "foreigners" or more precisely, Normands who form the contingent of William, the Duke of Normandy's men.

3. See Bell quote in note 1 above.

4. "N'ayant pu trouver leur étymologie, je place ici les expressions *belic* et *belif*, désignant en blason la couleur rouge et dès lors synonymes de *gueules*." André G. Ott, *Etude sur les couleurs en vieux français* (Paris: Librairie Emile Bouillon, 1899), 131.

5. Chrétien de Troyes, *Lancelot or, The Knight of the Cart (Le Chevalier de la charrete)*, trans. William W. Kibler (New York and London: Garland Publishing, 1981), 308; endnote 5770.

6. And because of the convoluted plot, the switch from the lady's banner is convenient in maintaining the ignorance of the four knights to the lady's love for each one of them.

7. Barker, *The Tournament*, 176.

8. Richard Thomson, *An Historical Essay on the Magna Charta of King John* (London: The Apollo Press, 1829), 284.

9. Pastoureau, 103.

10. Jacques LeGoff, *Time, Work, and Culture in the Middle Ages*, trans. Arthur Goldhammer (Chicago: University of Chicago Press, 1980), 161.

11. ". . . between the twelfth and fifteenth centuries, it becomes merely one of the processional dragons paraded almost everywhere in the liturgy of the Rogation days." LeGoff, 161.

12. LeGoff, 176.

13. And lest we forget, in the *Tapisserie de Bayeux*, the dragons depicted "foreigners."

14. LeGoff 175.

15. Pastoureau distinguishes it as the most appreciated in the hierarchy of colors: "La plus appréciée est le rouge—la couleur par excellence—. . ." Pastoureau, 94.

16. ". . . vermeil signifie en vieux français <<*rouge vif*>>." Ott, 123. Although, I have found in subsequent dictionaries that *vermoille* is identified with

"légèrement rouge" (Greimas, A.J., ed. *Dictionnaire de l'ancien français—le Moyen Age*. Paris: Larousse, 1994). In context of the romance, I find *vermoille* more indicative of a *rouge vif* rather than a light red because Chrétien de Troyes is making every attempt to highlight his hero; the indication of a brighter color would aid in doing so.

17.   Ott, 22.

18.   Jacques Ribard, *Le moyen âge: Littérature et symbolisme* (Geneva: Editions Slatkine, 1984), 50–51.

19.   Ott, 136.

20.   "Vert étant ainsi associé à l'idée de jalousie, avarice, il en devient la couleur symbolique." Ott, 138.

21.   "La perception de *blanc* doit exercer sur nos organes de la vue une sensation agréable, qui transmise à la partie *psychique* de notre être, donne lieu à un sentiment de *plaisir*, de *satisfaction*." Ott, 10.

22.   "*Blanc* symbolise aussi la *pureté*, l'*innocence*, signification qui ne demande pas d'explication." Ott, 10.

23.   Ribard, 51.

Chapter VII

The Lady and The Tournament

The idea of the medieval tournament typically evokes images of an ethereally beautiful woman sitting in the stands cheering on her beloved *chevalier*. Women were no doubt present at tournaments, particularly during the later ones where they became an integral part of the spectacle, but there is evidence that their association with the sport early on was more rare and more sporadic than usually believed; for example, in *Le Maréchal*, women are mentioned in just two of the sixteen events noted or recounted, and even then their role is rather restricted. When she is part of the tournament theater, as in several early medieval French fictional accounts, the lady's role is quite diverse; the lady's presence and/or role is frequently of particular importance to the tournament or its participants. In such works, women's characters are often developed beyond being merely devoted spectators. In this regard, women may assume a more complicated role and for example, conceive and organize the event. Other women associated with the tournament have an added dimension as jailers and judges in episodes peripheral yet crucial to a knight's participation in the contest. In one work, the hero appears most helpless and is totally dependent upon several women before he competes. Elsewhere, the lady's role is less complicated and visible but still vital inasmuch as she serves as inspiration for the whole affair.

"Soon a gallery of ladies was an essential part of every well-ordered tournament."[1] Although this is a valid statement, the key word is 'soon' because it is not the case for the early tournament; ladies and maidens (*les dames* and *les puceles*) are explicitly present in only seven sources and in only seven tournaments being used here; ratios expected to be indicative of other contemporary sources. In addition, the degree to which they are mentioned varies greatly. In one case, in *Amadas et Ydoine*, women are only alluded to as part of a great crowd on its way to watch a tournament; there is a mixture of noble ladies and *bourgeoises*[2] ("et chevalier et damoiseles / Esquiier, bourgois et danseles" [vv. 856–857]). Since they have no more importance than members of a large entity, there is no further allusion to their presence at this tournament. In *Perceval*, the women spectators' function is more developed, in part because they serve essentially as "reporters." For forty-eight verses, on the first day alone, their conversations about the competitors are recorded and through them many details are furnished. The ladies watch and talk again the second day as well, and their commentaries throughout the entire tournament are an interesting feature providing insight into the whole affair. Similarly, in *La Charrete*, noble (*gentes*) ladies and maidens are present ("Dames et dameiseles gentes / i rot tant que mervoille fu" [vv. 5524–5525]) and chat among themselves. For this tournament, there is a great number of ladies present, a detail reiterated several times by the author to emphasize the importance of the event (e.g., "Ja sont assanblees les rotes / la reïne et les dames totes" [vv. 5575–5576]). It is so important it has attracted the interest of many noble ladies in addition to men. Women appear as a measure of sorts of the importance of a competition.

In *Ipomedon*, the presence of women spectators is found throughout the tournament scenes, but just who they are is oftentimes confusing and cloudy. This is because at the beginning of the account, the author notes that many ladies, maidens and daughters of princes are on their way to the spectacle ("Od lui i meine la reïne / E dames e meinte meschine / Ffilles de princes e de ducs" [vv. 3145–3147]). Based on this, one assumes they will all subsequently be present as spectators, yet from then on, only the central female characters, *la Fiere* and her attendant Ismeine, are shown observing and discussing any of the on-going action, and they are always alone, separated from everyone else. At one point, the Queen is presented with a gift and in the evenings she joins in discussions about the day's events, but there is no other clear indication that she ever watches. By contrast, in *Partonopeus de Blois*, quite a number of noble women are said to be watching the tournament, namely the maiden Mélior, her sister Urrake, Persewis (the daughter of the King of Milet), and the Queen. At various moments in the tournament passage there are references to these women, as well as to others. Elsewhere, in only one of Marie de France's *lais* is there mention of ladies watching such an event, and that is the lady in "Chaitivel." Because ladies were rarely alone in the Middle

Ages, it is safe to assume other ladies were present in this instance, but it is not stated explicitly. In the *lai* "Le Lecheor," the practice of tourneying is the questioned topic of a group of ladies, but there is nothing to indicate that they are ever present at a real tournament.

The presence of women associated with a tournament in *Le Maréchal* is even more difficult to ascertain, however, it appears that women are present, albeit in a limited role, in two of the sixteen.[3] A lady[4] comes forth just at the end of the tournament scene at Pleurs, so one can only presume she was there during the action ("Avint qu'une dame de pris, / De grant ovre & de grant afaire" [vv. 3042–3043]). The second tournament where ladies are surely present is at Joigny, when once again there is a very noble lady, in fact, a countess, who appears ("La contesse s'en eissi fors" [v. 3455]) with her ladies-in-waiting ("O lié dames e damiseles" [v. 3460]). The women join with knights in marveling at how magnificent a tournament this one has been:

Li chivalier e les puceles,
Les dames e les damiseles
Distrent qu'il n'i aveit mès fait
El tornei[e]ment si beal fait. (vv. 3517–3520)

The women's viewpoint is quite valued here and having watched the action, they can concur with the knights that it was a splendid affair. Besides these two instances, there are no mentions of women at other tournaments in the narrative.[5] While in none of the remaining works are women overtly mentioned, many times it can be taken for granted that they are physically present; case in point is *Erec et Enide*. The tournament is held three weeks after the wedding of the protagonists, and is obviously in their honor. Enide, however, is not actually mentioned as ever being in attendance.

So why then is there less emphasis on ladies watching and cheering at the early tournament than there is in later centuries? The lack of attendance of women spectators at the early tournament, is no doubt correlated to the rather chaotic nature of the sport itself at the time. In its infancy, there were no set rules for knights to follow as procedures nor were there as yet standard bleachers for spectators to sit. The competition was often held in an open field outside the city or castle walls, consequently, it would be difficult and dangerous for ladies to be closely seated. Hence, an understandably greater degree less of a presence than there was in the fifteenth century when constructed seating was readily available.

Occasionally the ladies who play a role in the sources are quite directly and actively responsible for sponsoring a tournament. This is significant because it is relevant to the thesis that women were acquiring a different status that began to develop in the eleventh century. Prior to the eleventh century and the advent of courtly love, the noble lady:

> . . .était reléguée dans une situation très inférieure. Ne pouvant porter les armes, elle était considérée comme mineure, exclue des cadres féodaux; dans l'entière dépendance de son père pendant sa jeunesse, elle passait ensuite, . . . sous celle de son mari; veuve, sous celle de ses fils ou du seigneur du fief qui lui imposait un époux de son choix. Au spirituel, elle n'était pas en meilleure posture, . . . c'était encore un homme, . . . qui devant Dieu en avait la responsabilité. Tout changea dans les dernières années du XIe siècle.[6]

Although it is cleverly worked into the narratives so as not to be blatant, there is tangible evidence in the twelfth-century works of an attempt to change the status of women. Such evidence is provided in the *lai* "Chaitivel," because there is little doubt as to the principal lady character's involvement in the entire affair. The indications are that it is she alone who desires the event, organizes it, has all the arrangements taken care of, and has the tournament announced ("Ot un turneiement crié" [v. 74]). There is no notion that she is dependent on any male, or on anyone else for that matter. Since she is responsible for the tournament, she is also thus, indirectly responsible for the subsequent deaths of three of her *druz*, although the knights do contribute to their own demise through their ill-implemented tactics. It could be argued then, that with the depiction of the lady as the sole sponsor of the tournament, Marie makes an attempt to illustrate women's capacity for independence. Yet, in the very era, such independence still deviates radically from the norm, and Marie must qualify her position at the end of the *lai* by showing how such a situation cannot yet be realized successfully. The initiative and dependence by the lady is marred by the tragedy and guilt which prevail at the closure.

The case for the maidens in *La Charrete* is also rather aggressive and interesting. In hopes of finding spouses, all the unwed, available women of the land decide to organize a grand tournament:

> Pristrent un parlemant antr'eles
> li dameisel, les dameiseles,
> qui desconseilliees estoient,
> et distrent qu'eles se voldroient

marïer molt prochienement,
s'anpristrent a cel parlemant
une ahatine et un tornoi. (vv. 5361–5367)

They are essentially in control of the organizational aspect of the event and are certain it will be held. They take charge, set the date, and make the news known in all the lands ("Sel feront savoir et crïer / par totes les terres procienes" [vv. 5374–5375]). While they do have to get permission from the lord of the land, King Arthur, it is not permission to hold the tournament, but permission to permit Queen Guinevere to see it ("lors li distrent qu'eles voloient / que il sofrist que la reine' venist veoir lor ahatine" [vv. 5392–5394]). As soon as the Queen is given permission to attend, the women send out the news that she will accompany them. Guinevere becomes a cherished possession because the maidens do not simply say she will be in attendance or will go to the spectacle with her husband; instead, they emphasize that they, the maidens, will take her to the event:

Tantost par tote la corone
les dameiseles an envoient
et mandent que eles doivent
amener la reïne au jor
qui estoit crïez de l'estor. (vv. 5410–5414)

Her very presence makes this tournament all the more special. Word of her expected attendance draws seven times the usual number of participants ("que por un seul en i ot set / don ja un tot seul n'i eüst / se por la reïne ne fust" [vv. 5518–5520]). Her presence, thus, is important because she is an attraction all wish to behold, and furthermore she adds an element of grandeur to an oftentimes bloody event.

There is really little doubt as to whose tournament it is in La Charrete; it "belongs" to the maidens as evidenced in the first place by their gathering together and deciding to have a tournament. Additionally, they have not asked King Arthur to allow the Queen to attend just any tournament, but rather "their" tournament, identified by the use of the possessive adjective "lor" in front of the word ahatine in line 5394 of the paragraph above. The author, lest we forget, repeats that the tournament "belongs" to the maidens, for example in the line "a nostre ahatine venir" (v. 5405) he again uses a possessive adjective "nostre" when the women are speaking. Decidedly, the tournament in La Charrete is very much centered in what the women do, and it proves to be a very important occasion for the story itself.

Interestingly, even though directly responsible, sometimes a lady's reason for holding a tournament is not all together altruistic and pure-hearted, indeed, though not shown to be nefarious, a woman can be negatively portrayed. Such is the depiction of one young maiden in *Perceval* who pushes her very own father, Sir Tiebaut, to compete against her suitor. In turn, she tells her young beau, Melianz de Liz, that she will not give him her love unless he undertakes to tourney against her father ("Prenez un tornoi a mon pere / se vos volez m'amor avoir" [vv. 4836–4837]), who incidentally, has raised Melianz as a son. She in essence bribes her suitor; this certainly is not a very flattering picture of a maiden. In *Ipomedon*, the haughty young princess of Calabria wishes to have a tournament held merely so she can marry the winner, whom she is certain will be her beloved Ipomedon. Perhaps with some glee the reader discovers she is absolutely devastated when an anonymous knight wins and initially is not believed to be Ipomedon. The lady in "Chaitivel" also appears to sponsor the tournament for rather selfish reasons since it is only according to the performances of four of her *beaux* that she hopes to choose one sole suitor.

Whereas the aforementioned women have a relatively active role in a particular tournament's being held, in other works, women are afforded a more passive role and are only indirectly responsible for its occasion. This is true of *Erec et Enide*, where Enide is partly responsible for the tournament because it is held as a celebration in honor of her marriage to Erec, but as already noted, there is no other direct indication of her role or presence at the event itself. In the *lai* "Guigemar," the evil lord Meriadus, plans to hold a tournament because of the lady whom he desires as a wife. He wants the hero Guigemar to attend this tournament so that he can be absolutely sure Guigemar is his rival in love, and then kill him. Meriadus' scheme fails, but all the same, the tournament is organized because of a lady, even though she is ignorant of it. In *Partonopeus de Blois*, the maiden Mélior is indirectly responsible for the tournament because of her celibate status. Unlike *la Fiere pucele*, Mélior does not come up with the idea for the tournament, but she is the ultimate prize offered to the victor. These women are distanced from any overt involvement in each story's contest, yet are an all-important aspect of the event.

One of the more "legendary" passive roles of the female is that of inspiration,[7] and it is not uncommon to find a maiden or lady as the source for a knight's inspiration.[8] Surely, this is why Lancelot hastens to compete. He knows his beloved Guinevere is to be present and he wishes just to see her if only from a distance—truly a knight deeply inspired by his love. In *Le Maréchal*, at the tournament at Joigney, ladies are described as very beautiful and in this light provide inspiration based on esthetics. While they do not help in organizing or preparing the tournament, they are the reason knights strive to do their best. In order to impress the women, the competitors excel:

> Li chivalier saillent des rens
> Contre eles [e] si comme il durent
> Molt lor fu vis qu'amendé furent
> Por la sorvenue des dames:
> Si furent il, quer cors & ames
> E hardemenz e cuers doublérent
> A toz asemble qui la érent. (vv. 3464–3470)

And they do put on a very good show because the author mentions four more times in the account just how well the knights perform because of the ladies.[9] This tournament is truly a festive affair, even to the point that many knights join in singing with the ladies.

The lady can be symbolically present and provide inspiration on the tourneying field by means of gifts or tokens (sometimes personal belongings) which demonstrate her love or friendship to the knight. Some of the offerings include a ring (*anel*), a sleeve (*mance*), and a banner (*gumfanun*), all of which fall under the general term of *druërie* ("Chaitivel," vv. 68–69). In *Amadas et Ydoine,* to signify her love for Amadas, Ydoine gives him her ring to wear ("Un anel oste de son doi, / ou sien li mist et dist. . ." [vv. 1262–1263]). She also gives him a silk scarf ("Une enseigne de fine soie" [v. 1356]), a linen and silk sleeve ("E une mance de cainsil" [v. 1358]), and a belt ("E une çainture a armer" [v. 1359]). Amadas, no doubt, carries or wears all or some of these in tournaments for inspiration; in fact, according to the romance, due to the succession of gifts Ydoine sends him after his departure Amadas is inspired and able to capture prisoners and horses:

> Ses rices drüeries beles
> Li renvoie souventes fois
> Et as guerres et as tournois,
> Aniaus, çaintures, guimples, mances
> De cainil ridees et blances,
> Pour ce abati cent vassaus
> Et gaaigna cinc cens chevaus. (vv. 1464–1470)

These tokens act as good luck charms for him, without them, it seems
unlikely that Amadas would compete so well, especially since, once he
believes he has lost her (because of her engagement to another), he
goes mad. Fortunately, he is cured of his insanity (incidentally by
Ydoine), and enters a tournament in Lucca where he is again guided
by his love for Ydoine. There is no mention at this tournament that he
carries any token of her love, but she is surely on his mind.

In *Perceval*, Gawain carries a dress sleeve given to him by the very
young girl for whom he competes. This gift is interesting in its presentation because of the way it was chosen. When the lass decides to
offer Gawain something, she first thinks of her wardrobe and is distressed when she sees what she has. She feels that a sleeve from her
regular clothing is not worthy enough of Gawain and she says so:

> Mes mes manches sont si petites
> qu'anveier ne il oseroie.
> Espoir se ge li anveoie,
> il ne la priseroit ja rien. (vv. 5366–5369)

The attention given to such a token is charming and is taken even
further since her father then intervenes and provides her with a sleeve
worthy of Gawain. It is elegant and rich for its material is of crimson
samite (*vermoil samit*), this she beseeches Gawain to carry out of
love for her:

> <<Mes portez por la moie amor
> Ceste manche que je tieng ci.
> —Volantiers, la vostre merci,
> fet mes sire Gauvains, amie.>> (vv. 5436–5439)

The type of love exhibited by the young girl is a pure and innocent
love, and while it is not a passionate one as witnessed between Ydoine
and Amadas, it all the same, serves as inspiration and cause for Gawain
to join the contest.

Elsewhere, in the *lai* "Guigemar," the hero wears a shirt with the
right side knotted by the woman he loves. One assumes that he would
have worn this item during the tournament had it taken place, but can
only speculate since the tournament was cancelled. In *Ipomedon*, the
mysterious knight takes a moment to pause beneath the vantage point
of *la Fiere*. His squire Jasun comes forth and hands him his lance
which to his surprise is now decorated with a red band, ribbons and
gold buttons. Unbeknownst to him, *la Fiere* had attached these decorations and handed the lance to Jasun:

Es vus Jasun ki a lui vent,
Baillee li ad une lance;
Une vermaille cunussance
La Fiere li ad envee,
Od ses deus mains l'out atachee
A la lance od plusurs freseaus
E a butuns d'or gros e beaus;
Mut fut l'enseigne bone e bele, . . .
Ipomedon la lance prist. (vv. 5001–5013)

Ribbons and buttons are significant as symbols of love or friendship and even admiration which is what she is expressing at this time. Whatever personal item that is easily carried or draped to flutter in the wind makes for a cherished token. In none of the other works is there any reference to women's tokens of love except for *Erec et Enide*, where an allusion to wimples and sleeves is rather vague and concerns no particular woman ("et tante guinple et tante manche, / qui par amors furent donees" [vv. 2102–2103]). In the biographical narrative there are no tokens of inspiration or love indicated, which does not necessarily mean they were absent, just not noteworthy enough to mention.

Conversely, just as women gave tokens to knights, during the tournament, knights, in turn, could express their love or present offerings to ladies. In *Partonopeus de Blois*, in a gallant gesture during the action, the hero offers his banner to Mélior: "Son gonfanon li a tendu, / Et Mélior l'a rechéu" (vv. 8337–8338). Knights also send less "romantic" offerings to ladies as signs of devotion or attachment such as captured horses or prisoners; in *Ipomedon*, the hero sends both at the same time to *la Fiere*:

<<Beaus amis, fetez mun present
A la Fiere de cest destrer.>>
Puis si ad dit al chevaler:
<<Par la fei ke vus me devez,
Tut dreit en cel chastel alez,
Deske la Fiere en cel danjun
E a li vus rendez prisun.>> (vv. 3730–3736)

One wonders what the maiden does with such signs of devotion, but they were no doubt more public displays of affection rather than true gifts to be accepted.

Besides the organizational role ladies may have had in the literary tournament or how they may have served as inspiration for knights to compete, there are yet other dimensions to their presence in or about a tournament. One such case is in *Amadas et Ydoine* where, in contrast to all the tournaments where knights compete out of love for a woman (for example, "Chaitivel" and *Ipomedon*), Amadas, one time does not compete precisely on account of his love for Ydoine. The first few times these two meet, Ydoine shows no love for Amadas and indeed rebuffs him. He is so distraught that, most melodramatically, he takes to his bed for an entire year ("un an tout plain gist en son lit" [v. 829]). At one time during the year, a tournament takes place and a multitude of people passes Amadas' lodging on they way to the event beseeching him to get up and join. He, however, is so love-struck and saddened by Ydoine's rejection that he prefers to stay in bed. It could be argued that this is a convenient excuse by the author to keep Amadas from competing since he has not been officially dubbed at this point, and for him to compete would be a bit out of the ordinary. Be that as it may, from a psychological perspective, Amadas is guided solely and violently by his passion for a maiden.

With regard to *Amadas et Ydoine*, I must digress to discuss a scene that does not involve an actual tournament but certainly is tangential to the sport. I refer to Ydoine's role in Amadas' tourneying career; she is actually the catalyst for it. Sydney Painter remarks that in this era "woman had edged her way into the mind of the feudal male and had elevated and enlarged her place in society as he recognized it. No longer was she merely a child-bearer and lust satisfier—she was the inspirer of prowess."[10] Ydoine is precisely an "inspirer of prowess," considering that after she realizes her love for Amadas, she pushes him out into the world of tourneying. She assumes the responsibility of enumerating Amadas' duties and telling him how he must act. She councils him to become a knight and to do so posthaste. He then must leave on adventures as a knight errant:

> Et au plus tost que vous porés
> D'armes avoir, les requerés
> Que il prïent vostre signeur
> Le duc, qui vous veut grant honeur,
> Qu'il les vous doinst si ricement
> Com il doit et a vous apen.
> Puis si errés de terre en terre
> Vostre pris pourcachier et querre. (vv. 1243–1250)

It is henceforth Love, i.e., Ydoine, that prompts Amadas to fight so well in tournaments whether she is present or not ("Ce fait Amors si l'enpaint / que il ne doute riens ne crient" [vv. 4412–4413]).

Another dimension for the female characters is, in essence, that of a commodity, no doubt precious, but still a commodity. In *Ipomedon*, the princess heir is associated with commercial value since the majority of the knights are more inspired by her as a designated prize and what it offers than by her beauty or true love. Even though the princess is reported to be lovely, the knights hope to win and subsequently obtain her hand in marriage which will give them a wife and realm at the same time. The same is true for the participants in *Partonopeus de Blois* inasmuch as they compete for the hand in marriage of the maiden Mélior, which will also provide them with a realm.

Women though, did not always serve as catalysts or inspiration for the event. In this regard, they may have the role of jailer and judge whose personal decision is vital to the hero and his participation in a tournament. Indeed, in *La Charrete*, it has been noted that Lancelot is inspired to compete in order to see Queen Guinevere, yet, he is most largely indebted to another lady. When Lancelot learns the news of the grand spectacle he is actually in prison. In a fortunate twist for the hero, his jailer's wife happens to be in charge of the domain while her husband is gone. She obviously judges him to be honest when he promises to return to his cell once the competition is over, and on this assessment permits him to go compete.

The hero Partonopeus is in a similar situation as Lancelot when he learns of the tournament which offers his beloved Mélior as the prize, but his scenario is more complex. He too, is in prison, but unlike Lancelot who appears to get to the tournament on his own, Partonopeus is really, totally dependent upon several women from the time he learns of the event up to a day before it begins. As luck would have it, those involved take on a highly active and aggressive role in getting the hero to the competition. For his initial preparation, the maiden Urrake procures all his necessary equipment. Then she and another maiden, Persewis, actually help him dress, taking care even to lace his shoes ("Les cauces de fer a cauciés, / Et Persewis li a laciés" [vv. 6809–6810]). Considering that armor was awkward to put on, and since he is alone, it is natural that they help him; in this capacity Urrake and Persewis assume the role generally undertaken by a boy squire. Having a boat ready and available, Urrake and Persewis then sail and accompany Partonopeus to the land of the upcoming tournament. What is curious is that Partonopeus had resigned himself to being a prisoner and thus can do no preparations himself. He depends upon the girls exclusively; and in fact, once left to his own resources, he is subsequently taken prisoner. At this point, for

Partonopeus as it was for Lancelot, while in prison, the wife of his jailkeeper allows him temporary freedom to leave for the tournament, also on the premise that he should return immediately after its conclusion. Certainly, as presented, without the help of Urrake and Persewis, the knowledge that Mélior is the prize, and the release from prison by a woman, Partonopeus would not have competed. Likewise, without the help and trust of the lady, Lancelot surely would have missed the event. In these two instances, the jailkeepers' wives have a crucial, albeit brief, role associated with the tournament, and have served as judges of sorts in choosing to decide the "fate" of the prisoners by allowing them to leave.

One of the more curious aspects of the portrayal of women in the tournament scenes is how they are referred to. Throughout most of the Middle Ages, people did not have surnames,[11] but, baptismal first names did exist; and yet, the women associated with the tournaments in question are more often than not, not called by any name at all. They are designated by aristocratic title or they remain anonymous, and if they are named, it is at a different occasion than the tournament theater. In *Amadas et Ydoine*, Ydoine is the heroine's name, and while this name is repeated often, she never attends a tournament of which we are aware. Another example is Queen Guinevere. She appears early in the romance, *La Charrete* (and in *Erec et Enide*), and is identified as Guinevere, however, not once during the 461 lines of the tournament passage is she referred to by that name, and she is certainly present, being, after all, Lancelot's "director." In contrast, in these very same 461 lines, King Arthur, Lancelot, and Melïaganz, among others, are called by their first names. None of the other females at the tournament in *La Charrete*—not an atypical text—is named either; the young messenger is a *pucele*, but otherwise is unidentified. In *Perceval*, the girls are *dames* and *puceles*. One of the two sisters is referred to as "la fille Tiebaut l'ainznee"; the other "la pucele as Manches Petites." With these two examples, the emphasis is on the father's name "Tiebaut" and on the fashion of the clothing "Manches Petites." In contrast, the most visible men therein are called by name ("mon seignor Gauvain," "Melianz de Liz," or "Gerin, le fil Berte") but there is never a proper noun for either of the girls during the tournament, just the identifying epithet.

If it were not so consistent, this point of discussion might well be considered trivial, but the absence of names appears in just about every source. The only maidens of noble nature continually named at the same time the tournament is taking place are Mélior, Urrake and Persewis in *Partonopeus de Blois*. In *Ipomedon*, the heroine does not have a name but is called either *la Fiere pucele* or the princess of Calabria, only her attendant Ismeine is named. In *Le Maréchal*, *la contesse* is probably the Countess of Joigny, but the latter name is not used; the lady with the pike is simply "une dame de pris." In the *lai* "Chaitivel" *la dame* who sponsors the contest remains anonymous.[12] The inordinate absence of feminine first names in conjunction with the sport is extremely puzzling especially if one considers that Chrétien specifically says in *Erec et Enide* how important first names are. During the wedding ceremony scene, he even professes that a woman is not married unless she is called by her own proper name:

> Qant Erec sa fame reçut,
> par son droit non nomer l'estut,
> qu'altremant n'est fame esposee,
> se par son droit non n'est nomee. (vv. 1987–1990)

Enide's name is then given (line 1993), but as stated earlier, she is not mentioned as in attendance at the tournament which follows, and other women as well are not mentioned except nebulously. Perhaps Chrétien de Troyes explains the reasons to a degree with this short detail, then it would make more sense that in *Perceval*, the maidens are not called by their names because they are not married. But in *La Charrete*, however, there is still puzzlement since the author does not follow his own council as stated above because the Queen is married to King Arthur, yet, she is never called by "son droit non" during the tournament. Once again, observations lead to questions rather than answers.

Pertinent to the question of naming women of noble stature in conjunction with the tournament is the tension between the authors' presumed desire to keep women in a subordinate position, and their recognition of the increasingly elevated status of women. Women of this era did not enjoy much freedom and were subjected to rules formulated and laid down by men. As Carl Stephenson says categorically: "The position of women during the Middle Ages seems to have been one of complete subordination."[13] This attitude of subordination is reflected, even if unwittingly, in the scarcity of names, and as well as in the manner that women are generally presented in the tournament scenes in question. No matter how important women are to the development of a tournament, they are most often relegated to the background, serving as pleasing decoration. In the instances where their roles are more than ornamental, they are overshadowed by the performance of the hero in the contest or by the competition's outcome. Even in the cases where the women are the pretext for or organizers of the tournament, they ultimately regret their part, for, although they are initially in control, they cannot maintain their control over the event once the action starts (the one exception is Guinevere who has "control" over Lancelot, but had no organizational role). They are often sorely disappointed by the turn of events, as in *Ipomedon*, when *la Fiere* reproaches herself for having organized a tournament in which many of her friends die or are injured. In *Perceval*, the oldest sister loses control because she did not count on Gawain entering the fray; nor did she anticipate her lover's defeat. In *La Charrete*, at the end of the tournament, the prospective brides are unhappy because, contrary to their expectations, they have not been able to choose a husband. They were hoping to choose a husband according to the performances of the knights:

> les dameiseles, quant le sorent,
> asez plus grant pesance en orent,
> et d'ient que, par saint Johan,
> ne se marïeront ou an:
> quant celui n'ont qu'eles voloient,
> toz les autres quites clamoient;
> l'anhatine ensi departi
> c'onques nule n'an prist mari. (vv. 6049–6056)

They did not foresee the participation and closing reaction of someone as good as the Red Knight and must leave forlorn, no longer with things under control. Certainly, the lady in "Chaitivel" is unhappy with the outcome of her planning.

To view the attitude of the author towards women at a tournament is to find often an unfavorable one. The maidens in *La Charrete* are portrayed negatively when they all become jealous of one another after the Red Knight's good performance and do not know whom he may pick as an "amor" ("Et l'une est de l'autre jalouse / si con s'ele fust ja s'espouse" [vv. 6017–6018]). Earlier during the tournament scene the same women had been described as boastful. In *Perceval*, the author portrays maidens as gossipers and quite rude people for they ridicule and mock Gawain when initially he does not wish to compete. They say he is only pretending to be a knight ("mes il le se fet resanbler" [v. 5041]). The father Tiebaut says that his oldest daughter is extremely rude ("N'avez mie fet que cortoise" [v. 5390]); the author says another girl is foolish ("Une des dames celui fol" [v. 5086]). The little maiden is the only one portrayed as pure, and naturally, it is for her that Gawain participates.

Character portraits of women at a tournament are most assuredly, not always sweet and feminine, and the contrasts among them are noteworthy. The difference in character between *la pucele as Manches Petites* and her older sister and the other maidens has already been noted. In *Ipomedon*, during the tournament, Ismeine is more logical and calmer than *la Fiere pucele*. Noticeably, Ismeine's name is a true first name, not a nickname, and is not pejorative like the one of her mistress, the "Proud One." In *La Charrete*, the contrast between the Queen and the rest of the women is established by her relative quietness and attentiveness to the Red Knight. She sends out her orders to him, but otherwise does not discuss him with the other ladies. She has faith in him, although she is not certain of his identity, while the other females ridicule and make fun of him.

The maternal role of women is almost never mentioned in connection with tournaments. In just one event is any mother referred to at all, and then it is in reference to one of the knights. In *Erec et Enide* when Erec is fighting, a certain knight named Randuraz comes forth ("E Randuraz li vient devant" [v. 2144]). He is identified as being the son of an old woman: "filz la vielle de Tergalo" (v. 2145). Not only is the maternal affiliation irregular because knights are typically identified by their father's name, but it is just short of pejorative. His mother is not the "lady" or the "mother" of Tergalo, she is the "Old One," *la Vielle*. Nowhere[14] else does a mother's name appear nor are any women referred to in a maternalistic way in the tournament; yet, contrarily, fathers are ever-present and consistently alluded to during the game. Once again though, considering the way of life and the way women were viewed at this time, the exclusion of maternal ties should be of little surprise. There was no need to make any maternal associations because they would have served little purpose.

In conclusion, the twentieth-century author Joan Ferrante has stated that "one of the more striking features of twelfth century literature is the importance of female characters."[15] Female characters clearly can be important to the tournament when they appear in early literary representations of the event; some characters have a more developed and pertinent role than others. In general though, women received a relatively small measure of attention with regard to the literary tournament at this time. This is exhibited in the source material, even though they could be major forces in an event's organization or in encouraging a knight to participate. But while the ethereally beautiful woman may not necessarily be sitting in the stands cheering on her beloved *chevalier*, it is evident she played a part, however small it may have been, in the early tournament and added one more element to its popularity.

Notes

1. Painter, *French Chivalry*, 50.

2. This is the modern word for *danseles* as provided by Jean-Claude Aubailly in the modern French translation of *Amadas et Ydoine*, p. 29.

3. The scholar, Noël Denholm-Young believes there is only one tournament in the biography which mentions the presence of ladies: ". . .—the only French tournament of the period at which the presence of ladies is mentioned—. . . ." 242. While this does help to substantiate my statement about the absence of women as spectators of the early tournament, according to my readings of the biography, there really are two.

4. Sidney Painter believes this lady is the Countess Marie of Champagne, but she is not identified in the text. See Sidney Painter, *William Marshal* (Baltimore: The John Hopkins Press, 1933), 39–40. As Painter says: "If the Marshal served a lady, his biographer neglected to mention it." Painter, *French Chivalry*, 137.

5. Indeed, women are mentioned rarely in the entire text; William's wife is noted only three times throughout the 19,215 verses, the third and last being at his death.

6. George Duby and Robert Mandrou, *Histoire de la civilisation française: moyen âge—XVIe siècle* vol. 1 of 2 vols. (Paris: Armand Colin, 1958), 132–33.

7. "The idea of the lady as the source of inspiration behind knightly deeds is present throughout chivalric history from the early twelfth century onwards." Richard Barber, *The Knight and Chivalry* (Ipswich: The Boydell Press, Ltd., 1974), 71.

8. "The knights were willing to accept the desire to honor a lady as a plausible and honorable motive for fighting. They had no objection to admitting that love could improve a man's prowess. They could even be persuaded to believe that a knight should devote some attention to pleasing women and should treat them with comparative courtesy." Painter, *French Chivalry*, 142.

9. See also vv. 3538–3542, v. 3524, v. 3548 and v. 3552 for more examples of how ladies inspired the knights at Tournament 8.

10. Painter, *French Chivalry*, 143.

11. "L'enfant ne reçoit qu'un seul nom de baptême. Ce n'est pas son prénom, comme nous disons aujourd'hui, mais son véritable, le seul qui lui soit indispensable et celui par lequel il sera désigné sa vie durant. Ce qui nous appelons "nom de famille" n'est encore qu'un surnom (nom de lieu, de métier, sobriquet), tout à fait accessoire, propre à l'individu et non à la famille. . . . Dans

les textes, les personnes sont les plus souvent désignées par leur nom de baptême suivi de diverses indications d'origine, de résidence, de fonction ou de qualités." Pastoureau, 16.

12.   In "Chaitivel," though, there is less of a discrepancy in the way that the author treats the sexes because the men are not named either.

13.   Carl Stephenson, *Medieval History*, 3rd edition (New York: Harper & Brothers, 1951), 209.

14.   With the exception of "Gerin, le fil Berte" in *Perceval*. Here though, Berte could as well be the father's name and not solely the mother's.

15.   Joan M. Ferrante, *Woman as Image in Medieval Literature* (New York: Columbia University Press, 1975), 1.

Chapter VIII

Weapons and Techniques

Owing to the militaristic origins of the tournament, the weapons used in the twelfth and early thirteenth centuries during the competition were essentially the same as of true war.[1] Decidedly, the similarities are unmistakable, and there exist early visual battle depictions that show older, but without a doubt the same, weapons as those described in later tournament-related literature. One such example is again the *Tapisserie de Bayeux* into which are hand-stitched pictures of lances, maces, arrows and swords, all of which can be found in chronologically later literature. The techniques employed by the competing knights, whether of precisely how to wield a weapon or how to conduct oneself, were also those occasioned in battle. Knights had to rely on their knowledge of wartime techniques because there were no newly-devised ones unique to the tournament. Considering the precarious reputation the sport maintained at the time of the narratives, it is worth identifying some of the weapons and techniques referred to by the authors in order to determine whether they portrayed these two majors components with verisimilitude, or whether perhaps the writers depicted the *accoûtrements* with a less lethal nature than they actually possessed.

Whereas dwelling extensively on the particular weapons would serve little purpose, a brief list and supporting examples should suffice to identify the most prevalent ones in the works. The major arms as they appear, are the lance (*lance*), sword (*espee, espée*), and, because of its use in *Le Maréchal*, the mace (*mace*). The lance enjoyed the prime usage, typified in lines like these: "les lances ploient et arçonent" (*Cligés*, v. 4790), "et mainte grosse lance fraite" (*Amadas et Ydoine*, v. 4352), "e une lance en feutre tent" (*Ipomedon*, v. 5840), "lances levées ès galos" (*Partonopeus de Blois*, v. 7900), "lance baissiee, a esperun" ("Chaitivel," v. 97), and "lance levée el ranc se met" ("Doon,"

v. 224). The consistent reference to the lance occurs because the *mêlée* was the style of combat in the early tournament, and it normally involved the lance.[2] The sword appears over and over again as the second weapon of choice in the literary tournament: "meint coup i ot feru d'espee" ("Chaitivel," v. 106), "s'espee ensenglantee tent" (*Ipomedon*, v. 5862), "et de l'espee et de la lance" (*La Charrete*, v. 5972), "et il de lance et d'espee" (*Amadas et Ydoine*, v. 4409), and "e maint cop d'espée so[r] hiealmes" (*Le Maréchal*, v. 2951). Juliet Barker finds that the "secondary weapon of the *mêlée* was the mace,"[3] and in doing so, she suggests an inherent importance to the mace which is not supported by the works in this corpus. It is true that in *Le Maréchal* there are several references to this weapon ("doner de maces e d'espées" [v. 2510] and "e maint cop d'espée e de mace" [v. 2966]); however, by virtue of the number of times it is noted, it is placed in a tertiary role of importance behind the lance and the sword. The mace does not have much of a role in the other works either because it is not mentioned at all; for whatever reason, the authors of the fictional sources chose not to mention the mace.

The emphasis on specific weapons serves to enhance the scene's physical nature, and frequently, the scene is further enhanced by the use of certain verbs or adjectives paired with the weapons. A common pairing is with the verb *entreferuz/entreferu*; for example, in *Ipomedon*: "les lances abessent andui / e se entredunent es escuz / granz coups se sunt entreferuz" (vv. 4664–4666). Even in the much shorter *lais*, the associative verb matched with a weapon warrants mentioning by the authors for good reason ("granz cox se sont entreferu" ["Doon," v. 226]). The verb in these examples is a strong and explicit one, not only because it means to strike with a great deal of force, but also because of the image the root *fer* evokes—that of hard iron.[4] The proper verb or adjective, when wisely chosen, is sufficient to recreate the action and heated nature out on the playing field.

Arguably, the most crucial feature of the offensive and defensive systems of the sport, was the horse[5] and the techniques or talent it required to ride one. A particular type of horse was preferred because it had to be strong and able to carry a knight, be receptive to a knight's guidance, and be agile. Horses were also an extremely expensive part of the knight's trappings and the novice did not necessarily own one. To wit, in William Marshal's very first tournament, he believes he cannot enter because he has no horse. Naturally, he is terribly distraught at this prospect, but his patron at last procures one for him and he can participate. However, the horse in question is not well-suited for combat and is a wild one. Part of William's magnificence though, is the fact he can overcome the handicap of the unruly horse, tame it, and perform exquisitely at the tournament. The horse he uses is so unusual for a knight to ride in the engagement that the author mentions how no tournament had ever before been occasioned by such a type of horse not normally suited to combat. The horse played a vital role as part of a knight's equipment, and decidedly so since the equestrian element helped elevate the common foot soldier into a more refined combatant, as well as foster the noun cavalier (*chevalier*).

Naturally, there is an obvious distinction between equestrian knights and foot soldiers; yet, oftentimes, knights who began the tournament in the saddle ended up on foot. Men were frequently knocked off their horse ("li sodans est forment iriés / qu'il est abatus à ses piés" [*Partonopeus de Blois*, vv. 8115–8116], and "ja l'aveit cil lui si feru / que jus del cheval l'abati" ["Milun," vv. 417–418]). If knocked off the horse, a knight could continue fighting without automatically surrendering, but clearly at a disadvantage. At this point, a knight's skill was truly tested because the choice of weapon generally changed while on the ground. In such a situation, the sword was employed since it was more practical in close encounters[6] and when faced with awkward stances, which is surely the case for an unmounted knight vis-à-vis a mounted one.

When a knight was on horseback, he tended to employ the lance, although not exclusively, since the sword and mace were at times used.[7] The proximity of the opponent helped decide the weapon to choose as did other factors, such as the situation at hand. Partonopeus finds himself in a delicate situation just after he has just begun to compete; he has struck his opponent so fiercely with his lance that it breaks. Undaunted, he tosses away the lance and chooses a sword ("Sa lance a fraite et l'a jetée, / S'en vait ferir un de l'espée" [vv. 7933–7934]). Partonopeus then continues with the game. The spirited encounters do not cease merely because equipment is damaged or broken, and rightly so since, considering the fierceness of the competition, this was often the case ("ensemble justerent amdui / Milun le fiert si durement / s'anste depiece veirement" ["Milun," vv. 414–416]).

Whereas the lance and sword are the preferred weapons for mounted knights, when foot soldiers appear, as they do on rare occasion, they employ bows or crossbows.[8] There is a vague reference to many men at a tournament in *Le Maréchal* who one scholar determines to be foot soldiers.[9] There is, however, a clear reference to foot soldiers in the same narrative when Symons de Nëaufle arrives at Tournament 5 with three hundred of his own, fully armed:

> S'i estoit misires Symons
> De Nëaufle, qui out semons
> Treis cenz serjanz de pié o armes.
> O ars, o glaives, o gisarmes. (vv. 2827–2830)

The foot soldiers in this passage are carrying arrows (*ars*) and other weapons not normally used by the *chevaliers*. Cavaliers did not have the freedom to use both hands to maneuver a weapon; rather, they needed one hand to guide their horse. While foot soldiers could occasion a tournament, they are infrequently mentioned and certainly relegated to much less celebrated attention than mounted knights.

As has been pointed out, weapons used in the tournament were limited inasmuch as knights had to rely on those already in common usage, as well as those conducive to the *mêlée* style of combat. With regard to the necessary techniques employed, though, the knights were not terribly restricted. Of course, techniques such as how to hold a lance or a sword were obvious ones, but very few procedural rules or rules of conduct for the execution of the sport existed formally during the early years: "Peu ou point de règles: on suit son inspiration et on profite de ses avantages; toutes les armes, toutes les combinaisons, tous les coups sont permis. On se réunit à plusieurs contre un seul: aux habiles à ne pas se laisser isolés."[10] Another scholar concurs with this very observation and notes: ". . . nor were there any prohibited strokes as yet. . . . There was no rule to prevent several knights or foot soldiers from banding together against one knight. . . . Nor was it against regulations to arrive at and participate in a tournament which had already begun."[11] Such specifics as these scholars identify clearly show a lack of set rules for the early tournament; knights could do what they wanted essentially without penalty.

The very absence of precise regulations, which renders a portion of the event chaotic, helps distinguish it from the tournament of later years, and the above specifics and seemingly inappropriate behavior are supported by the sources. For instance, concerning the spontaneity of entry in a competition already begun, in *Perceval*, Gawain enters a tournament for which he had no notice prior to his arrival in the town hosting it; William Marshal and the Young King chance upon, and participate in, Tournament 4 in *Le Maréchal*. With regard to the notion of uneven numbers of contestants pitted against others, at one point, William Marshal is pounced upon by four knights ("entor lui en out plus de quatre / qui travailloent por lui prendre" [*Le Maréchal*, vv. 5008–5009]). Such an attack seems unfair and brutal, but curiously, earlier during the same tournament, William assisted by one friend, had boldly and fearlessly attacked these very four men, only at that time their group consisted of even greater quantities:

> Durement vint li Mareschals
> E sire Pieres de Preials
> Por asembren si asemblérent
> As Bergoingnons qui grant gent érent. (vv. 4993–4996)

In fact, William often found himself embroiled in similar fashion. In one of his first competitions, five opponents attack him without provocation ("cinc chevalier: al frein le pristrent, / en lui prendre grant peine mistrent" [vv. 1427–1428]). While it appears that William and his friend Pierre have chosen to seek out such odds, and while these situations did occur, it is highly unlikely that such odds were commonly sought out.

Varying, and seemingly impolite, accepted techniques are seen in the tactics of Philip, the Count of Flanders (curiously, learned from watching William Marshal). He would remain inactive, as though he were not going to participate, until he determined who was getting tired and/or gaining the advantage; then Philip would join the competition, charging fresh from the sidelines, and thus, catch combatants unawares:

> Li quens de Flandres se teneit,
> Qu'al torn[e]iement ne veneit
> Devant que tuit érent lassé
> E desrengiée destassé
> Quant il ve[e]it ses avantages,
> Comme cil qui ert proz & sages,
> Lor[s] lor moveit a la traverse. (*Le Maréchal*, vv. 2723–2729)

There are additional examples of similar tactics in the fictional narratives as well; in "Chaitivel," much to the chagrin and detriment of the four principal male characters, knights attack them from the sidelines ("Atraverse furent perdu" [v. 125]). In *Amadas et Ydoine*, just as the tournament at Lucca is apparently over, a fresh group charges out to do battle with the exhausted team on whose side Amadas is allied:

Tous arestés est li tornois,
Quant leur vint sus uns un grans conrois
Qui les acoellent maintenant:
Voellent ou non les vont menant
Jusqu'as lices mult laidement. (vv. 4353–4357)

In this instance, Amadas quickly defeats the group and saves the day. Decidedly, there was little to prevent knights from rushing onto the field of action, whether for a "bad" reason as reflected in those hoping to capture William Marshal or a "good" one, seen in the following source; in the midst of fervent activity, the hero of *Partonopeus de Blois* rushes out to save his comrade the King of France from sure capture by the Emperor of Germany ("Li vait ferir l'emperéor, / qui voloit prendre son segnor, / que contre terre l'a versé" [vv. 8681–8683]). Further reflection on this topic shows that more often than not, such behavior is inherently inappropriate and rarely succeeds. Furthermore, those who apply the devious techniques are generally anonymous figures or those whose personality and character are portrayed as equally unbecoming as the tactic itself.[12]

The particular technical aspect of unrestrained forays onto the fields of play was greatly due to the unrestricted terrain of the tournament[13] and occurred with more frequency than one would believe considering the danger undoubtedly involved in doing so. However, it is ironic that forays of the sort would take place since the nature of the tournament was to compete as a team, hence the great *mêlée*. A large part of the early tournament was the discipline[14] and camaraderie promoted by the teams. There was too much danger to separate from one's squad, to do so could prove detrimental to one's livelihood as the four central knights discovered in "Chaitivel;" they made a mistake and paid dearly for it:

Si quatre dru bien le feseient,
Si ke de tuz le pris aveint,
Tant ke ceo vint a l'avesprer
Que il deveient desevrer
Trop folement s'abaundonerent
Luinz de lur gent, sil cumparerent. (vv. 115–120)

The four strayed from their peers and were attacked by greater forces. Marie de France has a good sense of technical knowledge to recognize this mistake and is justified in passing judgment with her choice of the words *folement* and *sil cumparerent*. For future reference, she points out the dangers inherent in the lack of discipline.

The biographical narrative *Le Maréchal*, also stresses the importance of teamwork and discipline, and does so repeatedly: "Seréement & sanz desrei" (v. 1308), "Serré en bataille se tienent" (v. 1420), and "Serré & bataillé se tindrent" (v. 2498). In making comparisons between teams, discipline/order is often the emphasized feature of the narrative, and accounts for the superior nature accorded the English team in the text. The author stresses that the English stay together while their opponents are generally in disarray: "Li un correient a desrei / & li autre sagement vienent" (vv. 1418–1419), "E cil de la se desreérent" (v. 2499), "Mais cil tornérent a desbraz / qui trop orgoillosement vindrent / unques ensemble ne se tindrent" (vv. 2512–2514), and "Franceis vindrent a grant desrei" (v. 2802). Part and parcel of an orderly team was the horsemanship necessary to compete well, and in *Le Maréchal*, this is also duly noted ("Molt chevalchiérent sagement" [v. 1317], and "Aroté[e]ment chevalcha" [v. 1320]). It is due to obedience as well as talent, that the team of William Marshal excels; and certainly, for all knights, obedience was a key to surviving an early tournament which relied so heavily on teamwork.

The depiction of techniques in the sources is as accurate as modern scholars can ascertain: lances are lowered, "squadrons" charge, and one-on-one jousts occur. Men could enter when, where, and as they wished because there were no firm guidelines to the contrary. The techniques required for the sport were familiar to the knights because of their existant military origins. The poets knew that their readers understood the sport, and regular maneuvers were often taken for granted and not overly mentioned, whereas improper techniques and mistakes were underscored.

It was necessary for the poets to impart to their readers the significance of making mistakes in a tournament because the consequences could be dire. The poets certainly recognized the danger inherent in the weapons, as well as the ability required to maneuver well. These two major components of the tournament are portrayed with verisimilitude in the narratives and one comes away with a good idea of the talent needed to compete.

Notes

1. Modern scholars are aware of this and repeatedly make note of it such as Juliet Barker, who says that "in the old *mêlée* style tournament of the twelfth and thirteenth centuries almost any weapons of war were permissable." Barker, *The Tournament*, 179. It is important, as well, to remember that these weapons were extremely sharp and not blunted or dulled.

2. "the most obvious feature of the *mêlée* style engagement was the use of squadron manoeuvres and especially the massed charge with lances couched." Barker, *The Tournament*, 19.

3. Barker, *The Tournament*, 179.

4. According to definition, the word comes from the latin "ferire." *Dictionnaire général de la langue française*, eds., Adolphe Hatzfeld, Arsene Darmesteter, and Antoine Thomas (Paris: Librairie Delagrave, 1920).

5. "Le bon cheval avait dans ce jeu plus d'importance encore que la bonne épée." Jusserand, 312.

6. "The primary weapon of the fighting at close quarters in the *mêlée* was the broadsword." Barker, *The Tournament*, 179.

7. "On emploie la lance, l'épée et la masse, suivant le moment ou l'occasion, faisant remplacer, si on peut, ses armes brisées, nullement protégé par ces prescriptions courtoises qui interdiront plus tard de frapper un chevalier déheaumé." Jusserand, 308.

8. "Bows and crossbows are mentioned in this period [twelfth and thirteenth centuries] usually, it is true, with disapprobation, but nevertheless these were the weapons of foot soldiers who were allowed to participate in hastiludes at that time." Barker, *The Tournament*, 179.

9. Although there is nothing to indicate as much, Juliet Barker comes to this conclusion in her book on the tournament in England, and I have not been able to figure why. *The Tournament*, 142.

10. Jusserand, 308.

11. Barker, *The Tournament*, 142–43.

12. William Marshal is vindicated and absolved from shame when he uses the same tactic because he does it to help the Young King.

13. This is further explored in the chapter on location.

14. "The key to success on the tournament field was discipline. . . . Confusion meant vulnerability." Barker, *The Tournament*, 20.

Chapter IX

Location and Duration

Two elements of the tournament which are not often discussed are its location and duration. Perhaps this is due to the notion that both are inconsequential or dull, however, the tournament appears in some very interesting settings, both topographically and geographically, throughout the selected works. Sometimes it occurs in places that can be located on a map, and other times in legendary locales such as the Arthurian realm. The question of how many days a tournament lasted is just as varied and interesting.

In purely topographical terms, the event is normally held in an open field or plain.[1] These topographical locations, amongst others, *plainnes* and *praeries*, are constantly referred to in lines similar to the following: "desoz Tenebroc an la plaigne" (*Erec et Enide*, v. 2099), "Si sont plainnes les praeries / et les arees et li sonbre" (*La Charrete*, vv. 5608–5609), "Es plains devers Osenefort" (*Cligés*, v. 4543), and "Dunt par la plaigne erent plusur" (*Ipomedon*, v. 3578). Considering the wide expanse afforded by fields and plains, it is natural that the sport would be practiced there, and since the early tournament consisted of two large teams facing one another, there would be an obvious need for vast areas. The nature of the particular field is at times recorded as in *Partonopeus de Blois* where the field is all in bloom ("el pré flori") or in *Amadas et Ydoine* when the knights contend with a field of heather (*bruyère*) ("Qui ains ains parmi la bruiere" [v. 4456]). Before the action, the site is pristine and this is often duly noted. In *Le Maréchal*, the setting is described as "En un liu delitos e bel" (v. 3444). The beautiful, delightful, and flowering fields are interesting because they suggest springtime, thus allowing scholars to temporally place such engagements, but also, they provide a glimpse of how the area looked before the action. Decidedly, the fields do not look the same during and after the competition, in fact, they are often described as cluttered with carnage and injured *chevaliers* after the fact.

There occur at times, playing fields not free of obstruction, and curiously, instead of choosing another area of play, knights ignored the irregularities[2] or used them to their advantage, as William Marshal does in Tournament 10 of *Le Maréchal*. In this tournament, the situation unfolds near an abandoned tuft of ground which has been surrounded by a ditch and a spiked barrier called an *heriçon*[3] ("fors qu'une viez mote i aveit / qui asez ert de povre ator: / de heriçon ert close entor" [vv. 3934–3936]). A few members of the opposing team retreat to this area and tie their horses to the *heriçon*. William follows and also climbs up ("Encontremont la mote vint" [v. 3950]) capturing at the same time two of the opponents' horses. Because he recognizes the advantage of being separated by the "irrégularités du sol" he climbs down and out of the ditch with his newly gained horses only to, in turn, have them wrested away by two additional knights who come upon him from the opposite direction. The ditch was first a place of refuge, then a hiding place for William to reconnoître the scene, and finally, a means for him to acquire two prized possessions. Even though William's plans eventually fail, the scene shows that the lack of level ground for a playing field did not warrant cancellation of the competition nor was it a hindrance to the knights.

While the open expanses of the fields seem very far removed from inhabited areas, it was quite the contrary, and the fields are often located in front of villages or cities, which may be named, as in "Chaitivel"—"Que devant Nantes la cité" (v. 73), or unnamed, as in *Amadas et Ydoine* when the people are heading out of "the city" to watch—"De la vile issent mult grant gent" (v. 854). Whereas the cities may or may not be identified, inherent is the notion of a populated rather than a desolate area. Some cities became longstanding favorites for tournament locations, as in *Le Maréchal*, where three are held at Gournei and Ressons, and two each held near Anet and Sorel, and near Epernon. The preference for a specific urban center is further evidenced by tournaments being held in the same city in two completely different narratives. The said area is Lagny, in the Île de France area of France, where, first, in *Le Maréchal* a tournament takes place. Secondly, in a relatively obscure poem by Huon d'Oisi entitled "Le Tournoiement des Dames,"[4] the lady-competitors all journey to Lagny to tourney: "Lez damez tournoier vont / a Lagni" (vv. 6–7). Apparently Lagny was a good locale, perhaps due to the field, the courtesy of the people, or because of its location, but no matter the reason, it was often chosen.

Another city which hosts a tournament in separate works is Mont St. Michel, in northwestern France, which appears in the *lai* "Milun" by Marie de France, and the anonymous *lai* "Doon." In "Milun," the knights have all gathered for the engagement, "Al Munt Seint Michel s'asemblerent" (v. 385), as they do in "Doon," "Au Mont saint Michiel en Bretaingne" (v. 216). Besides being cross-referenced in the two *lais*, Mont St. Michel presents a unique situation because the town and the monastery (both called Mont St. Michel) are built upward on a three-hundred foot rock. At high tides, which occur twice a day, this very rock becomes an island. There are presumably few, if any, broad open areas on the *mont* on which to hold a tournament. This suggests that the competition was held on the rock's surrounding banks, yet they are no less hospitable for when the tides are out, the perimeters are sand-like; in places, this sandy area is even composed of dreaded quicksands. The tournament in "Milun" and "Doon" must take place on the sandy banks when the tide is out and not on the steep rock foundation of the island, and this terrain would naturally increase the degree of difficulty of the competition. The authors were no doubt aware of the maritime conditions of Mont St. Michel so the choice of this location is no accident, but it is fascinating for its difficulty. Aside from the treacherous terrain at Mont St. Michel, choosing it as a location for the engagement is further puzzling because it is principally a monastery, and the Catholic Church forbade "hastiludes" at the time of these *lais*. With this in mind, one could argue that to a degree, there is a sense of defiance in these two particular *lais* in placing an unholy activity in an extremely holy locale.

Just as the locations of the tournaments in "Milun" and "Doon" are of a marine nature, most of the other locales in the fictional works are near water, as in *Perceval*, where the tournament is held in a field in front of the castle at *Tintaguel* (Tintagel). The castle or city of Tintagel is located in the southwest corner of England, just over 1/8th of a mile from the Atlantic Ocean. In *Erec et Enide*, the tournament is held at *Tenebroc* (Edinburgh) which is about two miles from the Firth of Forth. The most detailed tournament in *Amadas et Ydoine* is at Lucca, or about twelve miles from the Ligurian Sea; the story's unnamed tournament is in the environs of Dijon (Ydoine's hometown), near the Saône River. In *Ipomedon*, the tournament takes place at Catanzaro, which is about five miles from the Ionian Sea. The tournament in *Partonopeus de Blois* takes place at Chief d'Oire[5] which is near a port, as the author indicates: "et sa nef arrivée / qui est de Chief-d'Oire assez près" (vv. 7750–7751). Generally speaking, most, but not all, of the source tournaments described take place close to the same body of water—that being the English Channel. Many an illustrious tournament takes place in Normandy and Brittany, which are two north-northwest corners of France, bordering on the Channel. Considering the means of transportation in this era, the fact that tournament areas are close to water is better understandable because shipping routes facilitated travel; the tendency to hold tournaments in areas close to water is thus an interesting but not a completely surprising feature.

Though above are several tournament locations outside France, the majority of the narratives' tournaments were held on the continent, more specifically, as stated, in the Normandy and Brittany regions of France. This is substantiated in *Le Maréchal* which shows that at least nine tournaments are in Normandy, for example, Eu, Saint James and Valeines, and Anet and Sorel. The author of the biographical narrative hints at a specific continental preference when he says that a knight must go to Brittany or Normandy to tourney, "En Brutaingne ou en Normandie / por hanter la chevalerie / o par tut la ou l'om turnei[e]" (vv. 1543–1545). Michel Parisse discovers a more exclusive preference and says, "La littérature situe les tournois entre Loire et Meuse avant tout. Champagne, Bourgogne, Normandie et Picardie sont des lieux priviligiés, mais les régions voisines se montrent aussi accueillantes."[6] The tournaments briefly alluded to or detailed in the *lais* of Marie de France (who is recounting folklore from Brittany), naturally, generally but not exclusively, take place in the Brittany region.

As it appears in *Le Maréchal*, the English preference for continental tournaments is rather understandable because the French were considered the best tourneyers of the day, and knew how to cater a good competition. The English chose to frequent tournaments in France, no doubt in part, because of their proximity with the continent, their historical ties to ruling houses of France, and their sheer desire to learn.[7] For a long time, the English had no choice but to search out tournaments in other lands because up to King Richard's legalization of the sport, not only were the Catholic Church's edicts upheld in Britain, but King Stephen had himself banned them in England. Richard I did not give tourneyers free reign, however, and limited the permitted tournaments to five areas[8] in order to better police the sites. Remarkably, during the period of ban in England, and in apparent defiance of all the edicts by the Catholic Church, France on the contrary continued to enjoy the success of tournaments.[9] Even with all the negativity associated with it, the sport had far reaching influence. In *Ipomedon* and *Partonopeus de Blois*, there is evidence of just how extensive the popularity of a tournament went; in *Ipomedon*, knights who hail from all over the known world journey to Calabria. To wit, the King of Denmark, and those of "Gutland," "Horkenie," Norway, Iceland, and Scotland are in competition. King Daires comes from Lorraine; King Ismenun from Germany. From Flanders, Spain, and far away "Ruissie" knights assemble. In *Partonopeus de Blois*, knights who travel to compete include the Emperor of Germany, the Sultan of Persia, and the King of Syria (*Sirre*). More exotic places are Bagdad, Mecca, Sicily, Libya, Elide, *Puille*, India, and Egypt. These far-away destinations indicate that the tournament was a universally practiced sport of the day, and it was not exclusively western european.

The locations of the source tournaments are generally in Europe which really comes as no surprise since the corpus is made up of Anglo-Normand French narratives, and chivalry as we are using it was essentially a European concept. In the romances of Chrétien de Troyes the events take place on the island of Great Britain and more specifically in the Arthurian realm, the supposed realm of Logres. This realm poses problems for scholars since the existence of Arthur and his world cannot be proven with certainty; in fact, Erich Köhler remarks that the Arthurian court is found nowhere, and that it is impossible to locate in the real world: "La cour d'Arthur, située nulle part . . . un royaume idéal impossible à localiser par rapport au monde réel."[10] He is correct to an extent when one speaks of the *court* of King Arthur, which may be idealized and impossible to locate in the real world, but there is better evidence to support the existence of what is known as Arthur's *kingdom* itself.

Most assuredly, the tournament sites named in Arthur's kingdom are in the real world, and for the most part, can be readily located on a map. Within the legendary realm of King Arthur, in three *romans* there are tournament locales in actual geographic spots still in existence in the modern day. These places are not "impossible à localiser par rapport au monde réel" and they are, Edinburgh in Scotland, and Tintagel and Wallingford near Oxford in England. What perhaps escapes, or at least bothers Köhler, is that Chrétien links the legendary world with the known world and makes them harmoniously co-exist in the romances. Real and imaginary territories are juxtaposed to form the Arthurian realm. The tournament in the fourth romance takes place between Pomelegoi and Noauz, two locales which to date, have been "impossible à localiser" in the known world[11] and cannot be referenced with any certainty. The city of Noauz is very important to the *La Charrete* romance because it has a double meaning and it sets the tone for Lancelot's performance in the tournament.[12] Even though quite difficult to locate, without the real or supposed existence of these two places the tournament could not be portrayed as it is in *La Charrete*.

Having treated the topographical and geographical settings of the tournament, the "architectural" or structural setting as it appears warrants consideration. As has been briefly mentioned, in the very early stages of the sport, the various divisions or limits of the playing field were defined in gentlemen's terms, that is to say, by honor, not by marked-off boundaries. The competition was most often held in a wide-open expanse[13] restrained only by natural boundaries. Such conditions were fine for the competitors but presented contemporaneous spectators with inconveniences since viewing areas or bleachers had yet to be a standard feature; spectators had to fend for themselves, often watching from a castle tower or wherever they could safely do so on the ground. In fact, one reason why holding a tournament in front of a city was often important, and actually necessary, was because it afforded spectators prime viewing areas. In the early years of the sport, the city provides ideal lookout points from rampart walls and from towers. It is from the top of the city bridge tower that the ladies will watch the action in *Partonopeus de Blois* ("As estres de la tor amont" [v. 7875]). If the playing field was in front of a castle, spectators also searched out the best spots for good views, as in *Ipomedon*, where *la Fiere pucele* and Ismeine see the unknown knight from the wall of the castle ("Ismeine al mur venir le veit" [v. 5846]). In *Perceval*, the maiden watches from a small tower ("d'une tornele ou ele fu" [v. 5474]), and in *Partonopeus de Blois*, spectators also watch from the castle towers. Most certainly, all were standing because specific seating arrangements were not a common feature and appear with little frequency in the literary works of the period; this is why an extensive passage on bleachers in *La Charrete* is so terribly interesting.

La Charrete is unique in its description of freshly constructed bleachers and Chrétien is most effusive in speaking of them, preferring to call them "lodgings":

La ou li tornoiz devoit estre
ot unes granz loge de fust,
por ce que la reïne i fust
et les dames et les puceles:
einz nus ne vit loges si beles
ne si longues ne si bien faites. (vv. 5580–5585)

Despite the apparent simplicity of these six lines, there are a great many implications in them. The fact that lodgings such as these had never been seen before ("einz nus ne vit") suggests that common twelfth-century bleachers were not very aesthetically pleasing or well-made, if made at all. Also, by stating that these are the longest lodgings ever seen, Chrétien suggests an increasing popularity of the sport, and an accompanying need to accomodate additional spectators. As for the material used, when Chrétien notes that the bleachers are made of wood (*fust*), he no doubt chooses the word for its rhyming capability, but in doing so he offers further detail about the construction which helps readers to visualize better the scene. Chrétien, a bit later in his "analysis," refers to the steps of the seating area: "einz l'atant au chief del degré" (v. 5903). Through this detail he enhances the description, but also reveals that some serious thought was being given to the comfort of spectators by positioning them up high to see the activity better rather than at eye level where it is difficult to have the proper perspective of the whole spectacle. As the sport gained popularity and evolved, seating became readily available, but in the early stages, whatever viewing advantage one had was limited, and with the exception of Chrétien de Troye's *La Charrete*, references in the sources to seating arrangements are few and brief. Naturally, the rationale behind bleachers, was to enable spectators to see and admire[14] all that goes on, but in doing so, such spaces create a closed-in area, thus limiting the playing range of the knights; consequently, although quite progressive and convenient, the early bleachers are a precursor of the numerous limitations imposed in later centuries.

While it took time for public comfort to be acknowledged, there was from a very early date a designated area of refuge for a knight. This area was called a *recet*,[15] a word adapted from, in a sense, the confusing word *lices*.[16] This area was a type of sanctuary, a place where a knight could rest without harm or fear of being engaged in some tussle.[17] Interestingly enough, on occasion the usage is confusing enough that it seems *recets* could be individual ones, and that each knight had his own, rather than being a large area for all to gather and rest; a good example of this appears in *Amadas et Ydoine*, where there are two examples of a *recet* indicating a personal refuge. The first occurs when Amadas has arrived at the tournament and shortly after comes out of "his" refuge, "De son recet ist Amadas" (v. 4254); the second example appears at the end of the tournament when night has fallen. At this point, the knights retire to "their" respective refuge, "A lour recet de deus pars vont" (v. 4552).

The word *lice* itself is not always indicative of constructed boundaries and its ambiguous use appears in *Amadas et Ydoine*. Towards the end of the tournament at Lucca, a fresh group of knights charges forth. Because of their quick attack, they push the opposing team all the way back to the lists: "Jusqu'as lices mult laidement" (v. 4357). Whether these lists are natural or ones constructed for the event is not evident, but it seems they are rather synonymous with *recets* because in this case they do not have any other indication.

The topic of the duration of tournaments truly is as interesting as that of their location, but can be treated more briefly. Among the twenty-seven actual tournaments under discussion, twenty-one can be shown to take place in one day's time. Three occur over two days, two over three days, and one over four days of activities.[18] None of the tournaments in *Le Maréchal* or the *lais* indicates a duration of more than one day, and one even finishes before nightfall, i.e., less than one full day. The duration of competition did not necessarily have to be decided and fixed ahead of time, and much depended on how the knights themselves felt after strenuous hours of action. In *Perceval*, the decision to continue the tournament a second day is made on the field only at the end of the first day's competition. The knights confer and agree upon this extension: "et au departir rafierent / que l'andemain rasanbleroient / et tote jor tornoieroient" (vv. 5130–5132). The engagements in both *Erec et Enide* and *La Charrete* also last two days, even though this detail is not given before the start. In fact, therein, the duration is just barely noteworthy since in *Erec et Enide* for example, a single line indicates this fact ("mes molt le fist mialz l'andemain"[v. 2217]). The spontaneity of such decisions clearly indicates the infancy of the sport since in later centuries little was left to spontaneity.

On the other hand, the length of competition could be fixed long before the event as in the cases of *Ipomedon* where it is announced four months in advance as a three-day tournament and *Partonopeus de Blois* where it is announced one year in advance as a three-day tournament. The competition in *Cligés* is planned as a four-day affair

("Qui devoit durer quatre jorz" [v. 4546]), but this detail is not provided much before the competition. Perhaps four days was a more common situation because in *Ipomedon* there is indication that three days is unusual. When the proud maiden decides on three days she recognizes her choice as going against the norm because she says: "E un turneement ci prendre / Ki sulement treiz jurz durast" (vv. 2492–2493). The word *sulement* tends to suggest that tournaments usually lasted longer than her choice of three days. Interestingly, when duration is tallied in this corpus, three and four days are unusual because one day tends to be the normal duration.

To conclude, each author appears well-informed about the lesser discussed topics of location and duration. To summarize the question of duration, in the *lais* and the biographical narrative, no tournament lasts more than one day; even the tournament at Lagny sur Marne in *Le Maréchal* which has over three-thousand competitors, does not last longer than a day. On the other hand, the romance narratives describe tournaments of a longer duration. All in all, the discussion of just where a tournament was held and/or how long it lasted helps the authors create the totality of the tournament and what it encompasses. As with the given asthetics of the fields in bloom, the reader can formulate personal ideas on how the scene looks and use the imagination. Just as they have done with other elements, the authors treat these details differently, but at the same time, they recognize the importance of each component of the affair, all of which reveals a highly adaptable and flexible sport, factors which surely added to its survival throughout the many centuries.

Notes

1. "... à l'intérieur d'une même province; non pas dans les grandes villes, mais près d'une fortresse solitaire, à la lisière de deux fiefs, de deux principautés. Ils n'ont lieu ni sur la place d'un village ni dans les lices d'un château, mais en rase campagne, en une lande ou un pré dont la superficie n'est pas limitée." Pastoureau, 134–35. This observation is also made by Juliet Barker: "It was fought over a wide area of countryside, often in a plain-. . . ." See *The Tournament*, 139.

2. "... les irrégularités du sol, les récoltes et les plantations sont de menus désagréments qui n'inquiétent guère ces batailleurs: . . ." Jusserand, 308.

3. Godefroy defines this as a "poutre armée de fer qui tourne sur un pivot et défend une porte de ville." vol. x. See "heriçon."

4. Huon d'Oisi, " Le Tournoiement des dames" in *La Poésie Lyrique d'Oïl*, eds. I.M. Cluzel and L. Pressouyre (Paris: A.G. Nizet, 1969), 37–45.

5. As stated in the romance's glossary, Chief d'Oire is the capital of the Oire region and is in France, but I have been unsuccessful in determining whether it is on the Loire or the Loir River, or if it is the modern city of Oiron. In her dissertation, "The Three Days' Combat" (Ph.D. diss., University of Chicago, 1931), Dorothy Winters identifies Chief-d'Oire as an "enchanted city" (14). This description leads one to believe Chief-d'Oire does not exist; however, I am not certain this is the case.

6. Parisse, 190.

7. "Just as Malory naturally turned to *the Frenshe boke* to tell him about the deeds of Arthur and his knights, so Englishmen looked naturally to France to teach them the way to stage tournaments in their own land." Barker, "English Kings," 213. Michel Parisse further notes the desire to compete in France: "La France est terre d'élection; l'Angleterre de Richard Cœur de Lion vient aux tournois beaucoup plus tard." Parisse, 191.

8. See Introduction on the background of the tournament for the exact locations.

9. "On sait que les tournois, interdits en Angleterre jusqu'à Richard Cœur de Lion, furent au contraire florissants dans la France du XIIe siècle, notamment au Nord et à l'Ouest." Chênerie, "Ces Curieux . . . ," 330.

10. Köhler, 38.

11. Some scholars have theories as to the location of Pomelegoi, e.g., "Brugger, ZFSL 28 (1905), 34, suggests that Pomeleg(l)oi might be identified with Linlithgow in Scotland." G.D. West, *An Index of Proper Names in French Arthurian Verse Romances 1150–1300*. (Toronto Press, 1969), 134. Louis-

Fernand Flutre's research places Noauz as a "château en Northomberlande ou en Cornouille." *Table des noms propres avec toutes leurs variantes figurant dans les romans du Moyen Age écrits en français ou en provençal et actuellement publiés ou analysés.* (Poitiers: Centre d'Etudes Supérieures de civilisation médiévale, 1962).

12.   William Kibler cooraborates this point: "Chrétien employs a pun which it is impossible to convey without changing the name of the town, Noauz. The expression, *au noauz,* can mean "Do one's worst" or "Onward for Noauz!" When Guinevere sends the girl to the unknown knight with this message, she knows that Lancelot alone, being the model lover that he is, will interpret it "Do your worst," whereas any ordinary knight would understand it simply as "Onward for Noauz!" Kibler, 307–308.

13.   "Guillaume le Maréchal affronte les troupes sur d'immenses espaces, près des villages . . ." Parisse, 191.

14.   ". . . il faut limiter l'espace où évoluent les combattants afin qu'ils soient vus et admirés." Parisse, 191.

15.   "Point de barrières entourant le champ de la bataille; les lices consistent en des sortes de barrages aux deux extrémités du terrain choisi, formant le *recet* ou lieu de refuge; . . . on y est en sûreté, on y reprend haleine, l'ennemi ne peut vous y poursuivre." Jusserand, 307–08.

16.   The word *lice* has an early definition associated with castle construction. It is a "band of ground" (*bande de terrain*), much as a moat, which encircles the castle (Pastoureau, 58–59). This definition of *lices* dates from the beginnings of medieval castle construction taking from the archetype for the medieval castle which appeared in the Carolingian period (768–987). In the late tenth century, some significant material and design changes took place, and new words were created to describe them. In my view, *lices* were some of these new changes, and thus this definition dates to approximately the late tenth century. This same definition is not to be confused with an even later one which applies to areas around the tournament field, occasionally referring to a resting area for knights and appearing in the literary works dated approximately 1180. For further clarification on castle construction and the "*lices*," see Pastoureau's Chapter 4 ("Tel Seigneur, Telle Demeure": Le Château et l'Habitat").

17.   *Recets* are further defined by Juliet Barker as "areas of neutral ground in which no-one was allowed to harm them [knights]." Barker, *The Tournament,* 141.

18.   In these numbers are days either solely devoted to fighting or days of fighting combined with preliminary procedures such as *vespres* or *començailles.*

Chapter X

Casualties

Molt metent sor lui grant entente
A lui grever e a lui prendre,
Mès n'osoient ses cops atendre;
Li plosor li leissent la place,
E maint cop d'espée e de mace
Donent al Mareschal Willealme,
Que tot li enbarrent le hialme
E li fendent trés qu'en la teste. (*Le Maréchal*, vv. 2962–69)

After reading a passage such as the one above, one would be convinced that tournaments were very dangerous and a threat to a knight's very existence. And, duly so, death was a well-known and highly probable consequence of the early medieval tournament. It was such a potential likelihood that even very early in their inception as a sport, tournaments were strongly criticized and forbidden by the Catholic Church. When tournaments were officially prohibited by the Catholic Church as early as 1130, it was fundamentally on the grounds that they were a form of "unjustifiable homicide."[1] They provided a dangerous theater not formally sanctioned by the Catholic Church as were the crusades. After this date, there were several amended canons,[2] but each re-emphasized the prohibition of the tournament because of its deadly potential. The Catholic Church obviously believed, as did many other critics, that tournaments were so physically and spiritually dangerous that they should be forbidden. Yet, despite the strong social criticism from, most vocally, the Catholic Church, and the possibility of death, the sport continued to enjoy great popularity among several echelons of society and in literature. It became such a standard chivalric event that it was easily assimilated as a widespread theme into contemporary literature, death not withstanding.

Since the Catholic Church openly condemned the practice, specifically for its perilous nature, and death was a well-known consequence, it remains that this result would be faithfully reproduced in such literature of the day, but the literary accounts of death do not always reflect the criticism voiced on the matter. The authors generally follow the same unspoken written rules in recreating the tournament and do faithfully reproduce it when describing aspects such as the weapons, maneuvers and terminology, but when the works are further compared, it is clear that death is not always depicted so faithfully and in the same manner. Truly, the depiction of death during the tournaments in several fictional works is diametrically opposed to its depiction in the biographical narrative. The evidence for this is that there are sixteen tournaments described in *Le Maréchal* and despite the often-described mayhem, severe blows, and occasional injury, not a single knight is reported as killed in any of the sixteen. In contrast, for example in "Chaitivel," *Ipomedon*, and *Partonopeus de Blois*, knights participating in a single tournament do die.

While we shall later show how death is shown, what is most puzzling in just about all the texts is that most of the time the reader must simply assume there are injuries; the authors consistently use terminology suggestive of injuries, but do not mention many explicitly; for example, in "Milun," there is not much information given because although the hero is knocked off his horse, he is not injured. Elsewhere, lines such as these from *Erec et Enide*, are not unlike those found in Chrétien's other romances:

> D'armes est toz coverz li chans.
> D'anbes parz fremist toz li rans;
> an l'estor lieve li escrois;
> des lances est molt granz li frois.
> Lances brisent et escu troent,
> li hauberc faussent et descloent,
> seles vuident, chevalier tumbent,
> li cheval süent et escument.
> La traient les espees tuit
> sor cez qui chieent a grant bruit. (vv. 2121–2130)

In this example, swords break (*lances brisent*) and men fall (*chevalier tumbent*), but this is just about as close as Chrétien comes to recounting injuries. He leaves the rest to the imagination of his reader.

The Arthurian romances in general are interesting to contrast with *La Chanson de Roland*,[3] where wounds and the like are portrayed quite graphically, e.g., "Fors de la teste li met les oilz ambsdous, / E la cervele li chiet as piez desuz" (vv. 1355–1356). Admittedly, *La Chanson de Roland* recreates a battle scene, but in many ways the tournaments in romances resemble a battle; the only real distinction is that tournaments occur in peacetime. To a degree then, when compared to *La Chanson de Roland*, Chrétien does seem to gloss over the injuries that must have been part and parcel of the sport. The question which then arises is whether the omission of graphically-precise bodily harm in Chrétien's Arthurian romances distorts the true nature of the event. The answer is, in my opinion, no, because, according to Chrétien's works that entail an engagement, the literary tournament did not depend on explicit visual evocations of carnage. The mere mention of certain items in conjunction with certain verbs or adjectives is sufficient to portray the violent nature of the sport: "hauberks torn apart" (*hauberc descloent*) or "saddles emptied" (*seles vuident)*. It is highly unlikely that Chrétien was not aware of the corporal harm possible from the tournament, but I believe he has chosen to ignore, in a sense, the horrors of the sport on account of his intended audience, and to a lesser degree, in deference to the literary genre within which he has chosen to work. His romances are intended to please; even in their day they were meant as pure entertainment. As a protégé of Marie de Champagne, he knew that his audience belonged to an elite society which did not need to be reminded of the bloody reality of one of its favorite pastimes.

In contrast with Chrétien, Hue de Rotelande wrote for such a heterogeneous people that veracity, as much as possible, was important.[4] This veracity—that is, a faithful rendition of what modern scholars assume reality to have been—is evidenced in Rotelande's work, *Ipomedon,* where during the three-day tournament there are many injuries to specific individuals and the hero himself is injured on the last day. Rotelande spares no words when he describes a certain knight as being struck in the chest, right next to the breast "Dreit en costé de la mamele" (v. 3660), another knight loses a few body parts. Rotelande is even more graphic in describing the brains and entrails that are strewn all over the field: "E meint boïlle i traïne, / e meint la cervele i espant" (vv. 3894–3895). By the end of the competition many knights die, and no one is above being killed because, tragically, fratricide even occurs. Albeit unintentionally, the young man Drias kills his brother Candor: "Cist est mi freres k'ai oscis" (v. 6069). Truly, death is not just alluded to or abruptly appears at the conclusion of the tournament narration in *Ipomedon*, indeed, words such as *oscis* and *mort* appear early in the account and continue throughout, leading to the conclusion that death was rather prevalent. Fatal blows are described in vivid imagery:

> Meint chef parmi esquarteré,
> Meint oscis e maint afolé
> E meint nafré par mi l'eschine,
> Meint feru par mi la peittrine. (vv. 4825–4828)

To Rotelande, these were true scenes of a tournament field, and to his audience, who obviously knew what the sport was really like, descriptions such as these, one must assume, were only natural.

The injuries spoken of in *Ipomedon* are quite explicit and seemingly necessary for the literary audience, but death and injuries are not viewed in the same manner by the characters themselves. Their reaction to injuries is more of awe. The greater the blows and the more helmets smashed, the more everyone is impressed by a tournament. There is little evidence that injuries are mourned very much, if at all, by the spectators or the knights, and this contrasts with their reactions to death. Despite all the carnage displayed in *Ipomedon*, the overall message Rotelande conveys is that death is not a goal of the game, and there is great sorrow when it occurs: "Li vif regrettent lez morz" (v. 3901). Even if death should happen to a rival there is no appreciation of the fact, for example, Ipomedon's rival, Amfion is killed, but there is no sense of satisfaction, only remorse at the casualty.

The narrative *Le Maréchal* provides further evidence that the intended audience of a work is a main factor in determining the nature of a literary tournament because there is an obvious lack of casualties. The terminology used does describe the general sights and sounds of the sport in such a way as to evoke the idea of corporal harm, for example, "Que il [i] out mainte testée / E mainte testière entestée / De coups d'espées et de mace" (vv. 3795–3797), but no one is reported dead, and specific injuries to named individuals are not generously given. Only a few times is anyone reported as hurt during the numerous tournament scenes and certainly no one is reported to have died. In fact, one of the recorded injuries is parenthetical to the tournament. Said injury is described in some detail because it is caused by William Marshal (the man in question is a thief and William pokes out one of his eyes). Another injury of interest that warrants a few verses occurs to a young knight on the team opposite William's in the last tournament of the biography. William is portrayed somewhat as a savior at this point when he rushes out to save the injured youth. We later discover this rescue was not altogether altruistic because William exacts payment for the young boy's freedom. However, since William exacts no further corporal harm on the youth, his reputation remains unblemished and the scene is worthy of a spot in the narrative.

Remarkably, William himself is never really injured in any of the sixteen tournaments despite the many blows he receives or often being at a disadvantage, for instance, in one tournament he is surrounded by four adversaries who do not inflict any bodily harm upon him, nor do they manage to capture him even though they greatly outnumber him. Even when he is hit, William seems invincible; once he received so many blows to his head that his helmet was bashed in tightly.[5] Yet, even here he is apparently not incapacitated and in fact, manages to get to a blacksmith's shop wearing the confining helmet. Hardy as he is, William allows the blacksmith to pound away with the helmet still on his head and appears unscathed. There is no indication he even has a headache.

The suggestive effects of this scene may be entertaining, yet, the lack of mortal injuries is suspicious. The lack of precision in what a modern author would call "realism," is in part due to the author's purpose of idealizing William's life for his audience. The omission of death protects the hero from accusations of being an accomplice to homicide and leaves his reputation untainted. It also lends little substance to the Catholic Church's condemnation of the sport for reasons of homicide. When presented in a favorable atmosphere, the sport appears less lethal, and it is easy for the audience to forget that the tournament could be deadly. One must conclude that the author manipulated the consequences to portray the tournament more as a sport where valor is the ultimate goal rather than a deadly one where a knight may perish. Given this reason, it is natural that the author embellish the virtues of the subject and minimize the tragic consequences of what was William's most frequented pastime, and actually, of what comprised his professional career. The fact that the author chose not to report numerous or any casualties during William's association with the sixteen tournaments provides strong evidence that he was, surely to some extent, concerned with the Catholic Church's criticism of the game, but even more concerned with maintaining the hero's highly esteemed reputation.

Whereas the numerous tournaments in Le Maréchal are described with no tragic conclusions, in the lai "Chaitivel" (as similarly in Ipomedon), the conclusion differs and three of the main characters die. On the surface the deaths are tragic and make the *lai* an ideal case in point for opponents of the tournament, as well as for modern scholars who feel Marie viewed the game negatively. The *lai* though, is not an erstwhile attempt by Marie to attack the sport of tourneying. While the knights' deaths are considered extremely unfortunate, and everyone is grieved by them, Marie does not criticize the knights for competing in a tournament. Rather, she prefers to criticize their technical performance, and focus on the psychological effect of the deaths not only on those who inflicted the deadly wounds, and on those milling about, but also on the remaining principal characters. In a passage worth printing, she focuses on the profound emotions experienced after the deaths:

> Cil ki a mort les unt nafrez
> Lur escuz unt es chans getez;
> Mut esteient pur eus dolent:
> Nel firent pas a escïent.
> La noise levat e li criz,
> Unques tels doels ne fu oïz!
> Cil de la cité i alerent,
> Unques les autres ne duterent.
> Pur la dolur des chevaliers
> I aveit iteus deus milliers
> Ki lur ventaille deslacierent,
> Entre eus esteit li doels communs. (vv. 127–139)

Thus according to Marie, two-thousand knights pull out their hair and unlace their helmets, such is their grief. The crying is so extensive that never had such sounds been heard before; the corporal destruction was hard to believe and all were distressed. Marie explains in twelve lines that while knights engage in brutal competition against one another, and spectators enjoy the action, no one wants to see someone dead or permanently wounded.

It is extremely important to recognize though, that Marie never once actually criticizes the sport itself nor holds it responsible for the dead. In fact, the actual human loss is not as great as what is gained from the deaths. From several additional interesting viewpoints there is much to be learned. From a technical viewpoint, Marie shows that the deaths were needless because if the knights had fought properly and not made a mistake, they most assuredly would not have died.[6] She speaks of the importance of working together as a team during a tournament. These four knights went off without the full corpus of their team and were attacked; inherently stating the importance of discipline. From another approach, the deaths appear to be morally instructive to the lady who organized the event since she is at least cognizant of how foolish she has been to subject four men to tests because of her selfishness. She does say she did not wish to lose them all just for the sake of one ("Nes voil tuz perdre pur l'un prendre!" [v. 156]), and in some manner does regret the loss of three ("Mes les autres treis regretot" [v. 179]). As a stylistic device, the death of the knights provides a solution, albeit tragic, to the lady's dilemma and for the eventual closure of the *lai*. Since three of the four suitors of the lady die, she no longer has to make a choice of which to favor; she is left with the maimed one. Of course, new problems arise, but her initial one of indecision as to who would be her favorite knight is solved through the tournament deaths. Finally, from a philosophical and metaphysical view, Marie instructs her audience that Death is the only eventual victor.

Marie de France wrote the *lais* to preserve Brittany's legendary past, but she also wrote at the royal court of Henry II of England, and therefore for an elite audience which she naturally would hope to please just as Chrétien de Troyes did. Granted, a *lai* is typically short, but it is in part for her elite audience that Marie does not dwell long on injuries nor go into graphic detail about the dead, she simply tells what injuries were sustained, just as someone would see it from the sidelines ("E li quarz nafrez e malmis / par mi la quisse e einz el cors, / si que la lance parut fors" [vv. 122–124]). Once again, we have an example of a narrative being written with the audience in mind.

In *Partonopeus de Blois*, there is just one tournament; it takes place over a period of several days, and many participants die. The manuscript does not survive in its entirety so it is impossible to determine accurately to what extent the author dwelled on the dead, but enough of the narrative remains that we know there are casualties. Interestingly, in what appears as a contradiction to a previous observation about "Chaitivel" and *Ipomedon*, while men die in *Partonopeus de Blois*, no one seems to contemplate sadly the dead or grieve for them. In fact, when the eponymous hero kills his jailer Armant, the tone seems to suggest that Armant's death is justified because earlier on the day of his death he had attacked the hero in an unknightly way. Moreover, Armant had been unfavorably described and introduced by the author, and thus with a similar lack of respect, he records no sorrow at Armant's death. In this romance, while it appears that the author is more interested in the trappings of the event than with its casualties, he obviously is not reluctant to describe the carnage, nor is there the impression that he is deliberately glossing over injuries or the dead as in Chrétien's romances or in *Le Maréchal*. The hero Partonopeus takes quite a few blows, as do many others; bones are hurt and bodies bleed ("Les os entirs et le car saine" [v. 8158]). If the author repeatedly interrupts the account of the tournament to talk about other things, it is because he is trying to manipulate the emotions of his audience for other reasons.

Death is recounted in *Partonopeus de Blois* in such a way that it ultimately appears natural at the tournament. The author does not dwell on the deaths as though they were out of the ordinary, and does not focus on anyone's grief to emphasize any dead. He concentrates on exacting emotions other than grief from his audience, for example, that of admiration at the chivalric talents displayed, or of hope for Partonopeus in his love quest for the maiden Mélior. The poet is not reluctant to describe death because he recognizes it as a side effect of the event. Deaths are mentioned because they most likely would occur and they enhance the veracity of the narrative; it would be suspicious and unrealistic to omit them.

As regards other works, the romance *Amadas et Ydoine* also is expressive in describing injuries and the deaths which occur on site. For example, by the end of the competition, there have been more than three-thousand blows to helmets and shields; many a brave knight lies on the field, and helmets, swords, and hauberks shine with the red that flows forth:

> Ci rot un estor si pleniers,
> De tronçons et de brans d'acier
> I ot feru troi mile caus
> Sour hiaumes st sor escus biaus,
> Si ot maint blazon destroé
> E maint blanc hauberc dessafré;
> Maint chevalier preu et vaillant
> I a contre tere gisant;
> Des hiaumes, des brans, des haubers
> Vole li fus vermaus et pers. (vv. 4501–4510)

Lances are broken, helmets are cracked, knights tumble to the ground. The colors of the flowing blood in the last line create quite an image of severely harmed bodies. The many knights (*maint chevalier*) who lie on the ground (*tere gisant*) are no doubt wounded, and quite possibly, mortally so considering the verb used is the present participle of *gésir* which is often associated with gravesites and death. No social status can prevent injuries: at one point, event the two team leaders lie on the field in a heap: "Que li doi cievetaine i sont / Par tere gisant en un mont" (vv. 4497–4498). The author is rather prolific with the passages and is markedly more graphic than Chrétien or the author of *Le Maréchal*.

Interestingly, it is not only human deaths which are discussed. Frequently horses were killed or hurt so severely they would be later destroyed. When a horse dies the authors take care to mention it, for example, Chrétien who remarks "et maint cheval i ot ocis" (*Perceval*, v. 5127). Horses were a very expensive commodity and a great deal of attention was given to them. Their death would be an enormous loss to a knight, and would be mourned by all.[7] It is curious that Chrétien takes care to mention the death of horses, but renders the tournament much less lethal towards man. Such seemingly unequal treatment stops short of suggesting that a horse is more precious than a human.

Considering that death was an obvious feature of the tournament, it is remarkable that the fictional works may portray it while the biography does not. The apparent biased representation by the biographer of such a noticeable consequence maintains that the intended audience of a work, is, if not the main one, at least one of the more salient factors determining how an author presents the sport and its various elements. The biographer of *Le Maréchal* attempts to downplay the most negative aspect of the competition to uphold his hero's reputation for future readers and for the son who commissioned the *histoire*, and at the same time to prevent further social criticism by proponents of the Catholic Church. The authors of the fictional works do not seem as constrained by the same social concerns as the biographer because their depiction of death, in addition to its realistic and literary value, oftentimes has a didactic value which outweighs the actual loss of life.

In reviewing the works and how death and the injuries appear, some interesting conclusions may be drawn; such as, the works provide evidence of the intrinsic bond between the intended audience and the work; some reveal this better than others, but truly, the question of genre cannot be separated from that of the audience. Also, while several works do not ignore the fact of death as a probable result, neither do any criticize the tournament as catalyst for death, consequently, they show no support for the Catholic Church's stance. What they may indirectly criticize is tactical error, as did Marie, or the loss of life as caused by someone's pride, seen in *Ipomedon*, but they do not appear concerned with the social criticism of death as the biographer of *Le Maréchal* appears to have been by totally ignoring the notion of casualties.

The tournaments in *Le Maréchal* occur as a "realistic" feature because they took place and William did participate in them, but they actually serve a greater purpose in his narrative, and that being to provide a plausible and rather pristine arena to display William's talents for future generations; the horrors of death would have served little purpose in such an arena. The authors of the fictional works, on the other hand, utilized the realities of death and injuries for reasons tangential to *vraisemblance*; the primary one being their didactic value.

Just as the tournament was an integral part of a knight's life and easily incorporated into contemporary literature, the fiction writers incorporated death into their tournament because it was a highly probable consequence. For his own reasons, the author of the biography chose to ignore it all together. This omission in no way diminishes the value of the biography, but scholars cannot ignore the evidence that the contemporary fictional works hold more true to life in describing the occurrence of casualties than does the biography.

Notes

1. Without any intent to provoke arguments, I would say that "justifiable homicide" occurred when knights were fighting in the name of God and for the Catholic Church. Although men were killed, there was supposedly a "good" reason to take the life of another. Tournaments on the other hand, took place in times of peace and none was defending God's honor, just his own.

2. A portion of one from the Third Lateran Council is reprinted here: *Canon*: Felicis memoriae papae Innocentii et Eugenii praedecessorum nostrorum vestiis inhaerentes, detestabiles illas nundinas vel ferias, quas vulgo torneamenta vocant, in quibus milites ex condicto venire solent, et ad ostentationem virium suarum et audaciae temere congrediuntur, unde mortes hominum et animarum pericula saepe proveniunt, fieri prohibemus. Quod si quis eorum ibidem mortuus fuerit quamvis ei posceni venia non negetur: ecclesiastica tamen careat sepultura. Cripps-Day, 39.

3. *La Chanson de Roland*, ed., Léon Gautier, 13th edition (Tours: Alfred Mame et fils, 1883).

4. The modern editor of the narrative remarks on how close Rotelande was to the people and how he and they had similar tastes for detail: "Hue de Rotelande était l'homme de son milieu. Attaché à sa patrie locale et formé par la vie troublée et exaltante de la marche galloise, il écrivait pour un auditoire qui partageait ses goûts et ses attitudes, et qui appréciait comme lui les petits faits divers de la chronique locale." Holden, *Ipomedon*, 11.

5. See verses 2966–2969 of the quote which opens this chapter.

6. See chapter on weapons and techniques.

7. "The horse was the most valuable booty to be won in hastiludes so that killing or wounding one was greatly frowned upon." Barker, *The Tournament*, 173.

Chapter XI

Tournament Winnings and the Victor

What could a knight hope to win by competing in a tournament? The awards knights could acquire by tourneying that were most relished in the early days of the sport were a widespread recognition of superior talent and an exalted reputation in the chivalric realm—gaining a highly esteemed reputation fundamentally through demonstrations of exceptional prowess. While other incentives were of course possible, most rewards of the early tournament were understood to be those which enhanced knightly characteristics such as *prouesse*, *largesse*, and *courage*. Naturally, to acquire and demonstrate these remarkable qualities, knights actively sought tournaments since they provided the means to garner and to extend one's renown.[1] Yet, in addition to personal rewards or attributes, on occasion, other more unusual and specific prizes were identified in the text and offered in the tournaments; among others, the hand of a maiden in marriage and a fish—more specifically, the pike. Interestingly, while they did attest to a knight's superiority among his peers, prizes did not necessarily have to be accepted at the event's conclusion.

A common general perception is that gains went solely to the male participants, however, the tournament, directly or indirectly, gave a great deal to women as well as men, for example, a lady could possibly find a prospective husband. If a lady gained nothing else, she might at least come out wiser because of the tournament. Occasionally, a lady might have an unexpected reunion with a long lost love, or be vindicated for some maltreatment. In most instances, specific prizes go unmentioned since the victory is often prize enough. The knight most apt to finish as champion was most often the hero/subject of the literary work in question, but on occasion, there is no true victor, and once, Death is the only one to emerge victorious. All these consider-

ations warrant a more extensive look, but before doing so, it is important for the modern scholar to recognize that the quest for honor and
glory was not perceived as haughty or egotistical in that long ago day
and age. Such a quest was an expected and accepted way of life for
the knights of the era, and we must not judge them too harshly from a
twentieth-century viewpoint.

Without a doubt, each of the protagonist-heroes, demonstrates great
ability and prowess at the tournament, and as a result, each gains
widespread renown. Historically, renown came to be considered an
element of successful knighthood since men talked about each other
at the *parlements* and the common people recounted tales of grandeur. What the successful knights also gained through their participation in a tournament—though they could have intended it only in historical cases, if at all—is textual immortality. Knights such as Ipomedon,
Amadas, Milun, and Partonopeus de Blois, to name a few, are the
subjects of narratives that perpetuate their names. In fact, thanks to
the narrative of his life, William Marshal is better known as a tremen-
dously talented knight rather than the undisputed, highly effective,
and well-liked Regent of England that he was for three years.

Eventually, the tournament became merely an occasion where a
knight was on parade; one of the main purposes of the game during
the late thirteenth century and beyond, was to show off one's magnificent costume; there was less thought given to actual talent or to being
highly esteemed by one's peers because of athletic ability. In earlier
years though, the tournament provided an opportunity to exercise, to
excel, and to compete in good company with peers. The tournament
was the necessary and primary locus where one could establish a reputation. Through his performances at tournaments in *Le Maréchal*,
William Marshal's prowess, valor, and generosity grow; as this example shows, he is held in the highest esteem by kings, as well as by
queens, dukes, and counts:

> Tant monteploia sa proesce
> E sa bonté & sa largesce
> Que de lui tenei[e]nt grant conte
> Rei & reïnes, duc & conte. (vv. 1901–1904)

Further evidence in this narrative points to the fact that not every
knight thought exclusively or consciously of material wealth. In the
following example, although he acquired great wealth from the sport,
William is quite unconcerned with material gains; his personal goal is
to perform well:

Mais al bien faire tant tendi
Que del gaaing ne li chalut
Il gaainna qui mielz valut
Quer molt fait cil riche bargainne
Qui onor conquert e gaainne. (vv. 3008–3012)

This portrait profiling William's humbleness is indicative of those throughout *Le Maréchal* because he is never shown to seek wealth actively through the event.

As mentioned previously, knights gained immortality by having their tourneying exploits written down. Most noticeably, and understandably, the biographical narrative *Le Maréchal* is dedicated to singling out such exploits. It excels in telling some sort of short episode, before or after the tournament which focuses on William and shows him in favorable light. For example, at the conclusion of the tournament at Pleurs (Tournament 6), several victorious knights refuse to accept the official prize. According to them, they would prefer to give it to William because he is more worthy than they. After extensive searching, William is found at the blacksmith's. Although this scene has little to do with the tournament itself, the author includes it with good reason. William's cool-headedness while the smithy hammers away, is witnessed by his peers and strengthens the idea that he can endure anything. A very favorable portrayal of the narrative's subject.

Other gains from the competition were more concrete than a reputation; these included money, horses or even prisoners (who later could be freed or exchanged for ransom money). In Tournament 7, William wins ten knights and twelve horses; the knights in turn must pay a ransom to William in order to be released. Once free, knights could re-enter the fracas if they wished, but at the risk of being taken again. There is one instance in *Le Maréchal* where William even captures the same man twice. The man had paid to be released after his initial capture, re-entered the game, and was taken again by William. And whether a knight paid a ransom depended on the knight who had captured him. For example, in Tournament 10, fifteen knights give themselves as prisoners to William ("Recevez nos: vos prisons somes / quinze chevaliers de compaigne" [vv. 4020–4021]), but he lets them go free without paying a ransom. We can only speculate as to why William is so generous in this case; perhaps he releases them because they surrender in a barn located off the playing field, or he may feel that they were not captured through a great show of arms, but no reason is given. Curiously, on another occasion, a captured knight returns to the playing field, not to participate, but to give advice. A certain William Malevesin had been taken prisoner by William Marshal early in the morning ("Qui ert prison dès le matin" [v. 5020]). Later, Malevesin goes out onto the field and councils four men who are trying to capture William Marshal ("Vint par iloec e si lor dist" [v. 5021]). The prisoner has such veneration for the marshal's abilities that he tells the four they are wasting their time. Certainly an interesting interlude in any day and age.

The narrative of the marshal's life has numerous passages of what the hero accumulates, but there are many examples in the other sources as well of what a knight could acquire. The types of gains were essentially the same (ransom, horses, or prisoners) and not all such acquisitions were covetously kept as some scholars believe; on the contrary, many of them were given away to other knights or to women. In the romance *Ipomedon*, the hero of the story captures a horse (*destrer*) and presents it to the young princess, using her cousin as intermediary. Erec, in *Erec et Enide*, wins many horses, but we are not told what he does with them, Gawain, however, gives away the four horses he wins (".IIII. en a le jor presantez / que il gaaigna de sa main" [*Perceval*, vv. 5520–5521]). Lancelot gives away any horse he captures ("et les chevax que il gaaigne / done a toz ces qui les voloient" [*La Charrete*, vv. 5982–5983]). Cligés takes many prisoners including Lancelot and Perceval, freeing all of them later. Amadas takes over fifteen prisoners, some of whom pay a ransom for freedom, while others choose to remain as part of his entourage; since Amadas is highly thought of by everyone it will be an honor to be associated with such a knight.

Ransom money for prisoners was not the only acquisition for William Marshal. He was prolific at winning, and during the two years William tourneyed with his partner, Roger de Gaugi, they won a great deal. One season, for instance, between Pentecost and Lent they took over a hundred knights, plus horses and equipment ("Qu'entre Pentecoste e quaresme / Pristrent cheval[i]ers cent e treis / Estre chevals, estre herneis" [*Le Maréchal*, vv. 3420–3422]). In fact, in the very first tournament in which he competes, he acquires money, equipment, three prisoners and various kinds of horses (*palefrois*, *roncins*, and *sommiers*). For someone who initially had to borrow a horse just to enter this his first event, these earnings are quite impressive and reflect how adept he was in the sport.

On another occasion, in addition to winning the day in Tournament 15, William is offered numerous unusual things by his friends. The Count of Flanders and the Duke of Burgundy want to give him five hundred *livres de rente*; the "avoué de Béthune" wants to give him a city and five hundred *livres de terre*; and Jacques d'Avesnes wants to give him a city, three hundred pounds and a percentage of all that he (Jacques) owns. These are extraordinary offers as gifts, and humbly, but graciously, William refuses all of them. He is content to be regarded as the best of the day. This tournament takes place relatively late in William's career when he was quite wealthy, so it is interesting to speculate on how he might have reacted had he been a fledgling knight. These offers signify that prizes did not necessarily have to be decided upon or designated before the tournament and they did not have to be accepted.

One of the more curious "forms" of payment by a knight is left behind at the tournament in *Ipomedon*; the injured Ismeun leaves an arm and an ear. Ghastly as it appears to us, the poet is not at all perturbed by this loss, but is rather amused and goes on to say it was more of a payment than necessary:

Tute l'oreille destre en prent . . .
Od tut le braz li fet le poign
Voler en mi cel champ mut loign; . . .
Ismeun mut tost se turna,
M'est vis trop grant guage i lessa. (vv. 3992–4004)

What is amusing to the poet is, no doubt, painful and heartbreaking for Ismeun, but not an uncommon occurrence.

The prior positive acquisitions were somewhat standard fare for the tournament competitors and hence, were essentially not publicized as available, but there were on occasion, specific prizes destined for the victor. Because the overt mention of prizes is relatively rare, the few instances one finds are of special interest, all the more so because only two specific prizes are designated throughout the sources: a young maiden as a potential spouse, and a fish. While the acquisition of a fish for the winner hardly seems impetus for knights to compete in a tournament, the prospect of marriage to a beautiful maiden is, on the other hand, the impetus for competition in two noteworthy fictional literary tournaments, those being the romance narratives, *Ipomedon* and *Partonopeus de Blois*. The tournament contained within each is conceived precisely for matrimonial purposes, and knights appear to compete solely for the prize.

Just as in modern days the decision to play is often contingent upon the available prize, usually in monetary form, knowledge of a potential prize other than knightly attributes could also be an incentive for knights to compete in a twelfth-century tournament. Knowing what prize was offered allowed the knight to be more selective in his choices, and as exhibited by the fictional narratives, the hand in marriage of a maiden was a strong attraction. This is certainly the situation in *Ipomedon* because more than 1510 knights compete. They do so essentially in hopes of becoming the husband of a beautiful princess. The tournament is arranged explicitly for marrying off the Princess of Calabria—*la Fiere*. She is a very haughty girl, and in fact, she is the catalyst for the game because of her haughtiness. She and her attendant, Ismeine, plan the idea of having the tournament and offering herself as the prize. She asks to have the event arranged because she expects her love Ipomedon to compete, win, and marry her. Her uncle along with the advisors to the throne agree it is a good idea to sponsor the tournament so she can reign with a man by her side who can protect the realm. They hope to find a worthy husband, and the victor of the event should possess the qualities indicative of such a noble knight.

To Ipomedon, the realization that *la Fiere* could be his spouse is the reason he travels from his area of southeastern Italy to Calabria. When the tournament concludes, considering that he has fought valiantly for the one he loves, Ipomedon should gladly receive his prize since he is the ultimate winner, but he is full of surprises. In another disconcerting move, he does not accept the prize at the end of the event. Ipomedon definitely sets up a dilemma; first, because each day the mysterious knight had won and everyone thinks there were three separate extraordinary knights. The *chevalier* in black on the third day is unanimously declared the victor. The dilemma continues because, secondly, even more puzzling to the spectators than the knight's true identity is the fact that the knight leaves the city after the tournament and does not stay to claim his prize. Ipomedon's unexpected rejection of *la Fiere* is most unsettling, especially when his true identity is discovered. Of course, much later, he does in a sense claim the prize inasmuch as he and *la Fiere* become a couple, but at the conclusion of the grand event, Ipomedon is not interested in carrying away the princess much to everyone else's consternation.

Just noted, *la Fiere* is the prize for the victor in *Ipomedon* and is indeed, directly responsible for the tournament. And while the beautiful maiden Mélior, heiress to the empire of Constantinople, is also the prize for the victor in *Partonopeus de Blois*, she, on the other hand, is indirectly responsible for the tournament. She does not come up with the idea of the game, it is a council of men that agree on the competition, but she is expected to marry the victor no matter whom he may be. As it was in *Ipomedon*, the purpose of offering Mélior as prize is to find a spouse for help in ruling the land.

The tournament and its prize in *Partonopeus de Blois* are announced a year in advance and thousands arrive; some even come from Libya, India, and Egypt. Yet, it is evident that the majority of, if not all, the knights are really anxious to compete in hopes of winning Mélior. Truly, most of the participants do hope to win her hand in marriage, some to such a degree that they act rudely. The fervent desire one knight has renders him boastful in front of all the other knights:

> Tant violt l'amor de Mélior
> Qu'il en est montés en essor
> Et en orguel si ranprosnant
> Qu'il vait tos cevaliers gabant:
> En ses amors a grant espoir (vv. 7965–7969)

His boastful nature is not a portrait of humility, and he is not victorious, but he is important as an example of what a proper knight should not do. The hero Partonopeus too, is inspired to compete when he learns his love is the prize, and after learning this news he must subsequently endure many challenges just to arrive at the field of play. He is an exceptionally talented knight and proves at the conclusion to be the best competitor. Happily to everyone's delight, he will gladly accept Mélior as a bride and she him, thus there is essentially closure of the competition at its end.

As previously noted in *Ipomedon*, *la Fiere* is not concerned before the tournament begins about her "status" as a prize because she is certain Ipomedon will eventually win the day. She is, however, distraught after the fact, and the anonymity of the three talented, yet mysterious, knights greatly distresses her. Since she believes Ipomedon does not enter the game (ergo the mysterious knights to be men other than he), she is very upset. Her betrothal to an unknown victor is a dreadful prospect because she is, after all, in love with Ipomedon and had not anticipated a different victor. Mélior is just as distressed about marrying an unknown as *la Fiere*. She believes Partonopeus to be dead and so "knows" he cannot be victor of the tournament. She too, is terribly distraught and cannot bear the thought of being the wife of anyone but Partonopeus. However, whereas *la Fiere* sees herself soon as the wife of a stranger, albeit a talented one, Mélior chooses a solution long before the event begins. She tearfully announces that her future will not be, simply because she will kill herself before marrying someone other than Partonopeus. Surely then, the possibility of becoming a total stranger's spouse could be disturbing to a maiden. The hand of Mélior as prize in *Partonopeus de Blois* is all the more interesting because there are pagans entered in the competition. If a pagan should happen to win overall, one of the conditions of the tournament is that he would agree to be baptized ("et se baptisera por moi, / qui pora vaincre le tornoi" [vv. 7165–7166]). Additionally, if a married man should win, he would give his prize—the maiden Mélior—to a designated friend. Mélior seems to have very little overt say in this decision which, fortunately, turns out in her favor.

The two fictional narratives provide a rather desirable prize, but such delightful acquisitions are not available to the victor in any of the tournaments in *Le Maréchal*. While conceivably a lady could find a prospective husband in a talented knight, and monetary and material gains could be incentive to compete, typically there is no allure for competing other than for reputation, joy, and honor in the biographical narrative. It is rather intriguing then, that in the sixth tournament in *Le Maréchal*, there is a prize given to the most valiant knight; a prize which is unlike the acquisition of horses or money ordinarily described. What renders this particular prize so unique is that a lady comes forth and presents a fish, or more specifically, a pike (*luz*) to a gallant knight. The poet takes care even to note its size: "Un luz qui faiseit a ami / De plus de deu[s] piez e demi" (vv. 3047–3048). At first, such an offering seems humorous but at the time, the pike was favorably viewed because it was believed to have talismanic powers. The modern historian Michel Pastoureau elaborates on this tradition and points out that the presentation of a pike as a reward to the most valiant and courtly knight was relatively common and most heartily accepted considering its mystical reputation: ". . . la plus noble des dames présentes remet au chevalier qui s'est montré le plus vaillant et le plus courtois dans la bataille une récompense symbolique. Dans les œuvres littéraires, c'est souvent un brochet, poisson qui passe pour avoir des vertus talismaniques."[2]

The whole sequence of this presentation is rather amusing. The initial recipient of such a noble prize is the Duke of Burgundy. He is presented with the fish but offers it to the Count of Flanders, who in turn offers it to the Count of Clermont, who in turn offers it to the

Count Thibaut, who offers it to another, when at last, it is the consensus among all the knights, that truly William Marshal had performed the best and was the most meritorious to receive such an honor. This decision made, William most humbly accepts the fish from his peers. Once again, the passing of the award from one man to another certainly shows that prizes did not have to be accepted by the initial recipient. In this story, the first one designated to receive the prize does not offend anyone in his courteous rejection of it unlike Ipomedon, whose non-acceptance of his prize, *la Fiere*, is short of scandalous.

In *Le Maréchal*, because the particular gift of the fish is not indicated prior to the commencement of the event, there is no anticipated excitement for its acquisition. Unaware of the award, the participants, no doubt then, entered to enhance their reputations, as well as to practice the sport. Therefore, the fish itself, unlike the possibility of marriage in *Ipomedon* and *Partonopeus de Blois*, is of little importance to the organizational aspect of the tournament. But, the *presentation* of the fish to the knight who has proven himself to be most valiant in the event (in this case William Marshal) *is* important to the work. Even though the scene is peripheral to the competition itself, it provides an ideal setting to show just how highly esteemed William is by his peers. A knight could have no higher honor than to be selected by his peers as the best. In contrast, in both the fictional works herein discussed, the mere anticipation of the prize is an important, in fact, crucial, element in the competition's organizational aspect and the tournament itself. Without the maidens offered as prizes in the romances, the tournaments understandably would most likely not have occurred or at least would have had much less thematic importance.

To this point, all the acquisitions from a tournament have benefitted the men involved, however, men were not the only ones to gain from the sport. There were possible gains for the ladies who attended as spectators. Some gains are more clearly manifested than others, for instance, the maidens in *La Charrete* organize the event expecting to gain a spouse. While these particular women are eventually disappointed because their plans are thwarted and, in turn, gain little from the tournament, other ladies or maidens who may be disappointed at the end of a tournament actually benefit since they become wiser. In the *lai* "Chaitivel," while the lady sponsoring the event is not especially repentant, she does appear to be cognizant of how foolish she has been to subject four lovers to tests merely due to her selfishness. Her recognition of the folly is manifested in the regret she shows even though it is directed more towards herself than towards the mens' deaths.

In the tale of *Ipomedon* though, the haughty princess openly gains wisdom. At the end of the tournament many of her friends die or are injured. The deaths are tragic, but the lessons learned from the dead are more important, and the deaths are greatly instructive; the young girl does regret the large loss of life. The deaths are an indirect result of her pride since she insisted on the tournament, hence, all the more tragic because the men died for someone's vanity. She laments having called together the spectacle purely out of pride. She realizes she has made a grave error, and clearly has learned a lesson since she profusely bewails her pride in a repetitively, and ironically, musical series of verses. In her words she cries:

> Ohi, orgoil, orible vice!
> Tuz tens pert la vostre malice;
> Par mun orgoil oi primes guerre,
> Par mun orgoil pert ceste terre,
> Par mun orgoil pert mes amis,
> Par mun orgoil a mort languis,
> Par mun orgoil, par mun desrai
> N'at mes nul hum cure de mei,
> Par mun orgoil sui desherite,
> De mun coup meismes sui chaeite. (vv. 4587–4596)

The repetition of *mun orgoil* emphasizes *la Fiere's* awareness of her culpability in the tragedy which occurred. The degree to which she dwells on this culpability reflects the grief she feels and the sincerity of her regret. Unfortunately though, it took a tragedy to teach her how wrong she has been; nonetheless, in the long run, she has gained. Ensconced in another somewhat unpleasant connotation for women is the possible acquisition of revenge which the little maiden of *Perceval* is able to gain on her older sister by having a champion defeat her older sister's beloved on the tournament field.

In more pleasant circumstances, if only indirectly, a few other ladies regain their lost loves as a result of a tournament. In "Guigemar," the hero is invited to a tournament. After he arrives at the proposed location for the event, a lady recognizes him as the lover she had not seen for many years and her fears of his death disappear. A similar situation appears in *La Charrete*; the Queen had heard that Lancelot was dead but during the competition believes she recognizes him on the playing field. After testing the Red Knight, the Queen knows he is truly her beloved Lancelot.

One other acquisition from a tournament which is not widely discussed by the poets, is the notion that knights could receive a type of salary during a tournament. Provided one belonged to someone's *mesnie*, one could conceivably receive a recompense. There is evidence of this in *Le Maréchal* where each man carrying the king's banner is paid twenty-five[3] sous for each day and each subsequent man he leads under the banner:

Quer qui unques portout baniére
E ert ove le giemble rei
A toz cels qu'il menout o sei
Aveient vinten sout lo jor. (vv. 4762–4765)

This is significant in itself because it is the only reference I found to knights of this period officially compensated for any appearances at a tournament. With the receipt of a daily sum of money the sport certainly takes on overtones of being a professional job of sorts.

The choosing of a victor of a tournament had less diversity than the gains did inasmuch as the victor is most often chosen by his peers, for it is they who have seen him perform in their midst. Generally after the end of the action, it is the knights themselves who gather together to discuss the feats of the day and in doing so eventually decide the overall victor. A good description of this procedure is found in *Amadas et Ydoine*:

A lour recet de deus pars vont
Mais ne parolent haut ne bas
De nule part fors d'Amadas:
Li pris li ont communement
Douné de cest tornoiement. (vv. 4552–4556)

The two opposing sides (*deus pars*) or teams, jointly give the victory to Amadas. From a psychological viewpoint this decision shows that the animosity (whether real or feigned) which fuels the two teams before and during the event, turns into a sense of camaraderie at the end. Such camaraderie among the teams in deciding the overall best must have been a relatively common feature for it is noted in *Le Maréchal* quite a few times (e.g., "De deus parz le pris lui donérent" [v. 5592]). To be chosen victor in any manner is rewarding, but is more special when done by one's peers.

In some of the tournaments, such as *Ipomedon* and *Partonopeus de Blois*, the competing knights are joined in council by other men such as advisors to the throne, in order to choose the victor. In

Partonopeus de Blois, there is actually a panel of judges who chooses
the victor; this council was no secret at the time of the tournament's
proclamation, and is no surprise considering a realm is at stake with
the marriage of Mélior. At the close of the competition on the fourth
and last day, the lady will pick out the best five, six, or more of the
participating knights; from this select group the judges will then choose
the victor:

> Au quart jor s'en eslirot six
> ou sept, ou huit, ou neuf ou dix,
> des plus vaillanz et des meillors
> si doint ma dame ses amors,
> o tot le nostre assentement . . .
> et de devant les jugéors;
> si esliront toz les meillors. (vv. 6599–6610)

Partonopeus is thus elected by the judges as winner ("Nos eslisons
Partonopeus [v. 9347]), but not all winners are chosen by such elaborate proceedings. In fact, in the narratives, the victor is more often
than not nebulously indicated as he who is said to "conquer" or "van-
quish" (*veincu*) the tournament itself or "has" (*avoir*) the prize (*pris*).
Some examples of such vagueness are as follows: "qu'il aveit le tornoi
veincu" (*Erec et Enide*, v. 2222), "et mes sire Gauvains a porte /
d'une part et d'autre le pris" (*Perceval*, vv. 5530–5531), "Cligés le
pris et le los a" (*Cligés*, v. 4658), and "Que li Mareschals out [le] pris"
(*Le Maréchal*, v. 3555).

In some works under study there is no true victor, not because the
author fails to mention one, as the author of *Le Maréchal* frequently
does, but either because no single knight excels over the others, or
the purported victor does not remain long enough to claim officially
the victory. As has been mentioned, Ipomedon leaves the city after
the announcement of his victory and does not stay to claim his prize;
his departure and essential rejection of the prize leave the question of
the victor in doubt. One could ask whether there is ever a real victor in
a tournament of this sort, considering the many dead and injured.
Indeed, Death appears to be the winner here. The romance *La
Charrete* also leaves the true victor in question. The unknown Red
Knight is chosen by both teams as the best competitor: "d'andeus
parz distrent sanz mantir / que n'i avoit eü paroil / cil qui porte l'escu
vermoil" (vv. 6024–6026). He leaves immediately after the tournament and does not officially accept a prize or public acclaim. Although
he has the private satisfaction of having obeyed the Queen, by leav-

ing, he dashes the hopes of all the maidens who wanted him as a husband (even without knowing his identity). The end of this tournament is thus portrayed as anti-climactic. In *Cligés* as well, there is no real victor after the tournament. Cligés has been able to defeat three splendid knights on each of the first three days, however, on the fourth he cannot best Gawain. Gawain and Cligés fight with equal verve and King Arthur is obliged to call for a halt: "Departi sont li chevalier / car li rois le vialt et comande" (vv. 4928–4929). Since they are equals, there can be no single victor.

A few of the other sources have tournaments where the victor is not terribly well proclaimed or is quite unexpected. Decidedly, in the *lais* "Milun" and "Doon" there may be two victors of the competition depending on one's point of view. For example, in "Milun," the young central character knocks the eponymous character off his horse. By rights, he is thus the victor of the tournament. However, at this very point in time, Milun learns that his young adversary is his long-lost son; in this manner Milun scores a personal victory. Marie de France makes no mention of an "official" victor in this *lai* because it is much less important to the story than the fact that no one really loses. In the *lai* "Chaitivel," the only one who really wins is Death. In *Ipomedon*, Death shared the winner's spot with the hero, but in "Chaitivel," Death is the sole victor having claimed three of the four main characters' lives ("Kar li trei i furent ocis" [v. 121]). The fourth valiant knight is sorely maimed and does not consider himself a winner in the least.

To conclude, knights obviously compete in the literary narratives for their reputations, for prowess and courage, but in the fictional narratives, at times such incentives were relegated to the possible espousal of a maiden whose hand in marriage was a prize which greatly inspired the knights. The offering of a maiden in marriage also added substance to the works by fostering the tournaments in *Ipomedon* and *Partonopeus de Blois*. In contrast to the fictional works, the participants in the sixteen tournaments in *Le Maréchal* compete, not for matrimonial purposes, but rather for recognition of their talents. The evidence for this lies in the fact that the nature of any prize is not given prior to the conclusion of the sport in any of its tournaments. This in itself is not unusual though because prizes did not have to be designated before the competition, but it does show that the incentive to compete had its foundation in chivalric endeavors. Apart from *Ipomedon* and *Partonopeus de Blois*, the authors seem to place less emphasis on the winner and the various concrete prizes than they do on the ceremonial award of honor and glory. They spend more time detailing an upcoming tournament[4] than they do in describing its outcome. It may be perhaps argued that the relatively small amount of attention given to the victor (seen in minimal one or two lines) is an attempt to refute claims that knights compete out of greed. Whatever the truth, there was a great deal to gain from a tournament and there were diverse kinds of winners; this is well revealed in the literature.

Notes

1. In fact, Lambert d'Ardre mentions in his family history that one ancestor, Arnoul de Guisnes, preferred to tourney rather than sit idle, because tourneying provided exercise and worldwide renown: "il aima mieulx frequenter joustes, tournois et nations estrangeres, que demourer oisif en son pais sans prendre l'exercice de guerre, affin d'acquerre bruit et parvenir à honneur mondain." Lambert, *Chronique d'Ardre et de Guines,* 204.

2. Pastoureau, 135. The offering of a pike fish was obviously a medieval custom unlike the offering of a maiden which appears to have been solely a literary custom.

3. Paul Meyer, the editor of *Le Maréchal,* translates *vinten* as "twenty-five," although it seems more likely to be the number "twenty."

4. See chapter on participants for a comparison.

Chapter XII

The Tournament as a Literary Device

Throughout the preceding chapters, great detail has been focused on specific aspects of the tournament as they appear in the corpus under study. It is now time to examine the probable reasons that authors recreated or even mentioned tournaments in their narratives, and to see how the tournament functions and serves as a literary device. Often the functions in a given work overlap; two of the most obvious are to show publicly the prowess of the main character and to enhance his prestige. The tournament can also be used to reunite characters, if only briefly, and it can be a test of faithfulness. As a literary device it can be vehicular and move the central character from one place to another. A scheduled tournament can be merely a ruse or it may be the occasion for exposition of viewpoints such as political and/or personal ones. It may offer a solution to a problem. In a few works the authors attribute moral significance to the sport and use it as a didactic device. There was a valid and natural spot in a lengthy knightly tale for the integration of the event, and tournaments do serve a purpose other than usage as fillers.

In an article concerning differences between the romance *Ipomedon* and the romances of Chrétien de Troyes, Lucy M. Gay observes that "half the poem is concerned with the tourney and the hunt, whereas the tourney in Chrétien is but an episode."[1] Ms. Gay is correct in her observation but fails to inquire further into the roles played by the tourney in each respective work. Another scholar, Michel Parisse believes that one of the reasons the tournament appeared so often in the literature of the day is because it was a popular diversion.[2] Logically, such a popular knightly pastime would be frequently reflected in chivalric literature; in this regard Parisse's belief is correct, but nor does he go further to consider *literary* reasons for the tournament's appearance. No author was obliged to write of the event, and one can see in the sources, when an author chose to describe a tournament, it was for a specific reason in addition to its being an historical fact. William Marshal's biography is revealing in this respect; the poet devoted nearly 7300 lines to the recreation of tournaments in the work, but most assuredly, it was not merely because the sport was popular or because it was just a large factor in William's life.

Primarily, the sport of tourneying serves as a gauge of a knight's reputation.[3] It is to be expected that the prowess of the principal knights is highlighted. Naturally, the locus of the tournament provides an ideal setting to establish or speak of the highly sought and regarded chivalric traits of *prouesse*, *courage*, and *largesse*, or to employ adjectives such as *preu*, *bon*, and *vaillant* in describing the protagonist. In the romance *Cligés*, for example, Cligés shows just how talented he is at the tournament, and is thus able to gain honor and glory. He does so thanks to his athleticism, and not through his relation to King Arthur, the sponsor of the event. Ipomedon too, in the romance of that name, shows his extraordinary prowess in the tournament and thereby gains honor for himself. Gawain, in *Yvain*, counsels Yvain and beseeches him to take up tourneying in order to increase his fame: "Or primes doit vostre pris croistre! / ronpez le frein et le chevoistre, / s'irons tornoier moi et vos" (vv. 2503–2505). In the sixteen tournaments of *Le Maréchal*, William is invariably seen as the knight with the greatest prowess; he is often praised by the other combatants: "Mais tuit loérent par egal / la grant proesce al Mareschal" (vv. 5589–5590). Even should they be lost at some point, one's honor and prowess can be regained in a tournament, as in *Amadas et Ydoine*.

Short episodes apart from but associated with tournaments are commonly found in the narrative *Le Maréchal*. These episodes offer extraordinary portraits of the hero. In Tournament 11, the poet mentions little about the tournament proper except where it will be, who will attend, and how the knights assemble. The interlude between the eve of the competition and the morrow allows the poet to tell the story of how the preceding night William maimed a thief who had stolen his horse. The next day's proceedings are presumably less exciting than the pre-game adventure because there is no further account of the competition. The same is true of Tournament 10 where little is said of the actual combat, but the author describes out-of-bounds encounters between William and other competitors.[4] In fact, each time a tournament takes place in *Le Maréchal*, its purpose is to aggrandize William, directly or indirectly. The exaltation of the hero in

Ipomedon is similiar inasmuch as the events leading up to the competition in this romance also prepare the subsequent subtle magnificence
of the hero and enhance his superiority over other knights.

Unfortunately, on the other hand, the tournament can be a cause
for disgrace, as in *Erec et Enide*. The game initially appears to be a
pure digression, a pretext for the poet to go into great detail about the
colors, banners, and other decorations seen at the spectacle. The scene,
however, is important in the plot because it is Erec's "swan song." It is
at this time that Erec chooses to experience the splendors of marriage
rather than the splendors of the tournament. Therein, the tournament
acquires thematic importance, instead of purely descriptive importance, because Erec's lack of interest in and absence from the sport
are cause for his disgrace, which in turn provide the substance for the
remainder of the romance.

Along with character portraits, the use of a tournament in a narrative can serve as a test of faithfulness or to reunite characters. Two
examples that use the game mainly as a convenient and realistic means
for reunions are the romances *La Charrete* and *Partonopeus de Blois*.
Also in each case, the identity of the hero is initially hidden, but his
lady recognizes that her beloved is competing right in front of her and
so the couples are to an extent reunited; in the *lais* "Milun" and "Doon"
the tournament serves to reunite a father with his son. In these situations, the sport is a plausible means of bringing people together. Without this means, there is hardly a logical way for the various groups to
reunite or to learn important facts. Even in *Le Maréchal* the tournament helps to reconcile people; prior to the competition at Gournei
and Ressons, William had been maliciously spoken of to the Young
King. Believing he has fallen out of favor with the Young King, William decides it would not be proper to enter this tournament. The
Young King, however, insists on William's presence and sends for him.
William agrees and goes to the competition where he then saves the
Young King twice from capture. The two are now seemingly reconciled.

With regard to faithfulness, nowhere perhaps, is it better revealed
than in *Le Chevalier de la charrete*, the tale of Lancelot. Lancelot is
rumoured to be dead, yet, manages to compete in the tournament
described therein. He is not openly recognized as Lancelot since he
competes in a borrowed red costume and all wonder who he is ("Trestuit
de demander s'angoissent: / Qui est cil qui si bien le fet?" [vv. 5634–
5635]). Lancelot's identity, however, is suspected by his beloved Queen
Guinevere, and she, suspecting the truth, sends a command to the

Red Knight ("et si li dites a consoil / que 'au noauz' que je li mant" [vv. 5644-5645]). Lancelot interprets the command as "to do his worst," and no matter how painful the consequences, he obeys, proving totally faithful to the Queen despite the almost dire results. It is not Lancelot's shield that Guinevere recognizes rather it is his faithfulness because the phrase has a double meaning and would have more commonly been interpreted loosely as "Cheer for the town of Noauz" whereas Lancelot understands it as the test of obedience it was meant to be. In much the same vein, the inclusion of a tournament further provides Lancelot, and elsewhere Partonopeus, with the opportunity to reaffirm their honest nature. Both are prisoners left in the charge of a lady from whom they must obtain temporary freedom should they hope to compete in their respective tournaments. They both do so by promising to return to the cell immediately after the tournament's end. Lancelot fulfills his promise and Partonopeus would surely have done so, but his captor is killed during the action and the widow grants him his freedom.

In the *lai* "Guigemar" the announcement of an impending tournament is used by the antagonist, Merïadus to entice the hero, Guigemar, to the former's castle. Merïadus wants to watch the reaction of Guigemar when the latter encounters the lady whom Merïadus suspects is Guigemar's beloved. The tournament here is an ideal means to lure the hero into a trap, but the scheme fails and, in fact, turns out to the advantage of Guigemar; the sport is used slyly in this instance. In "Chaitivel" the tournament is also a ruse to get four suitors together, but the ruse is motivated by selfish love rather than disdain for an opponent as it was in "Guigemar."

Each of the tournaments, quite naturally, serves as a vehicle to move the hero from place to place, however, its vehicular function is most often of lesser importance to other concerns and goes unnoticed. In "Le Fresne," though, the vehicular function is clear because no tournament takes place in this *lai*. Marie mentions a tournament in order to give the hero, Gurun, the excuse to stop at the convent where his love, Fresne, resides: "A un turneiement ala / par l'abbeïe returna" (vv. 249-250). One could argue that Marie refers to the tournament in a cursory manner merely to show how commonly practiced the sport was, and, to an extent, she does. But she gives it added importance by using it as a means of bringing together the hero and heroine.

The tournament can have political, social, or, albeit rare, even religious connotations or it may express prevailing attitudes on such matters, either attitudes of the characters or of the author. As previously discussed, in *Ipomedon* and *Partonopeus de Blois*, a whole realm's future depends on the tournament and its outcome considering the heiress in each is to marry the victor. In *Amadas et Ydoine*, feudal opposition is visible when two feuding barons schedule a tournament, ostensibly as peers and men of high status:

> Car mult erent li doi baron
> de haut afaire et de grant pris
> mais por itant, ce m'est avis
> que il erent andoi per mal
> de lonc d'une were mortal. (vv. 1582–1586)

Doubts concerning the sincerity of their friendship lead the King of France to realize that, once in the contest, the two men will no longer fight as peers, but instead, will be mortal enemies; consequently a true deadly war (*were mortal*) could break out. The tournament is then cancelled because the king understands the political implications of such a confrontation. Through the amicably-based sport the barons hoped to have fought out their differences, but their plans have been thwarted. *Le Maréchal* also contains tournaments that have sublime political implications because the participants are often listed as the English competing against the French, and the author frequently belittles the latter.

There are not only political implications in the biography, but also long commentaries by the poet revealing his own views of then-current practices. For example, in Tournament 11, in a long tirade, the author praises the Young King for having brought back chivalry:

> Li halt home si com il durent
> Quer, si com ge vos ai conté
> Par la proece e la bonté
> Del giemble rei e de son pris
> Out chascuns endrei[t] sei enpris
> A meintenir chevalerie
> Qui ore est molt près de perie . . .
> Si li reis Henri[s] d'Engleterre
> Poeit en pais aveir sa terre
> Que chivalerie e proece
> E bonté de cuer et largesse
> S'en istreient parmi sa porte. (vv. 4298–4317)

The poet discreetly equates *chevalerie* with the sport of tourneying. The Young King, he says, was able to maintain the art of chivalry by participating in as many tournaments as possible. His presence in a perishing, forbidden sport helped sustain it until it became legal in certain territories, and enjoyed a resurgence in practice. The remark that "chivalry is near perishing" (*près de perie*) mirrors the course of the narrative because the year in question for the Young King's delight in the sport is approximately 1180, a year when tournaments were not legal in any land. It was not until 1194 that King Richard I legalized tournaments in England. These noted lines reflect personal views of the author because there is no indication that they are uttered or thought by any character. The poet's positive attitude towards the sport of tourneying, encased in a flattering portrait of young king Henry, stands in opposition to the Catholic Church and its negative opinion of the sport, and is a subtle yet interesting endorsement for the knightly recreation.

Personal opinions on tourneying are likewise expressed in the *lai* "Le Lecheor." The passage does not concern an actual tournament, rather the sport as a whole is questioned: "Par cui sont li bon chevalier? / por qoi aimment a tornoier?" (vv. 32–33). These lines presuppose a feminine challenge—"Why do knights like to tourney?"—to the ideals of male-dominated chivalry because the poet places this question in the minds of the finest women of Brittany. Admittedly, the tournament is not the only male activity questioned, but this skepticism concerning a major practice of knighthood, often carried out to honor women, is particularly striking inasmuch as it represents a supposed female viewpoint.[5]

With regard to the religious element of the tournament, only quite infrequently is religion invoked with any connection to the event, for instance, one poet mentions that knights attend mass prior to the commencement of the action, but that is the extent of the notice. In truth, the tournament scenes are not marked by religious terminology, images, allusions, or expressions of belief. The conflict between the sport and canon law was a sensitive subject of the day; poets tended to avoid it in their treatments of this thoroughly secular activity. One poet, however, broaches the topic, but quite prudently; this particular poet is the one who wrote *Partonopeus de Blois*. Religious implications are found in the naming of participants for the eventual contest because they are offhandedly identified as Christians and Pagans: "Or avons dit de crestiens / or vos redirons de païens" (vv. 7201–7202), yet, interestingly, one of the judges, Ernols, makes the decision to have a non-pagan leader for each side. As he says, if the teams remain divided by religious indication[6] and fight in the tournament against each other, it would be war and not a tournament: "Ce seroit guerre et nient tornois" (v. 7183). The King of France is thus to lead one side and the Emperor of Germany will be the opposing leader, hence any religious conflict is diffused.

All these works illustrate that while poets may note opposing religious or regional affiliations of participants, knights must unite as friendly adversaries in order to compete. This is significant because it touches on one of the main differences between a battle in a war and combat in a tournament. An important element of the tournament is that it was undertaken in peacetime by peers, equals; no one better or different at the onset of each tourney; no one openly hostile to another. Moreover, death was decidedly not one of its goals, whereas one could easily argue that death is a goal of battle. One of the goals of the tournament was not to destroy an opponent but to build one's own reputation through high quality and superior maneuvers.

One of the more important functions of the literary tournament is to serve as a solution to a problem. On occasion the solution may be simply some form of elimination of the problem; other times it is more complicated. In *Partonopeus de Blois* and *La Charrete*, the tournament is a solution to the heroes' dilemma of captivity, from which they are granted either temporary freedom in Lancelot's case, or through the elimination of his antagonist, total liberation for Partonopeus. Furthermore, thanks to the tournament, there is a solution for dispelling the rumors of each hero's death. The tournament in the two *lais* "Doon" and "Milun" solves the namesakes' problems of their filial quests since each father finds his son. The *lai* "Guigemar" also uses a tournament to reunite two lovers and thus solves their problem of ignorance about each other's whereabouts. In "Chaitivel," the tournament provides a solution, nonetheless tragic, to the lady's problem. For Amadas, the hero of his own romance, the tournament solves his problem of ineptitude. He is once again able to tourney and regain the honor he had lost. The tournament in "Le Fresne" solves Marie de France's problem of plausibly allowing Gurun to locate Fresne because he passes the abbey with a legitimate reason. Even in the narrative *Le Maréchal*, problems are solved through the sport. For example, just prior to Tournament 4, the English team of the Young King is in a quandry because it is not adept enough to win tournaments. William comes along with his talent for tourneying and becomes a member of the Young King's team. From then on the royal

English group wins; these successes solve the Young King's problem of never having won at the game.

The inclusion of a tournament scene in a narrative can further be important by serving as a didactic device. As such, it can prove morally instructive to a character such as *la Fiere pucele* in *Ipomedon* who awakens to her sin of pride through the event she helped establish, or morally instructive in a different way for the lady in "Chaitivel." The poet of *Le Maréchal* additionally uses the tournament scenes as subtle technical lessons in his frequent referrals to discipline and horsemanship. The poet further delights in making technical comparisons between the "mesnie" of the Young King, i.e., William's team, with opposing ones. Truly, there was much to learn from the literary tournament and the poets provided or "taught" lessons in entertaining and hardly pedantic ways.

The tournament provides the poet an ideal occasion for contrasts which are seen first, in virtually all the works when the hero in some manner associated with the competition, furnishes a contrast to everyone else at that time. When the hero competes, through his talents and virtues, he bests all competitors. This is most prevalent in *Le Maréchal* where William competes in numerous tournaments; invariably, he is superior to the others. But throughout the works, there are other contrasts associated with the sport between hero and supporting characters; for example, both Cligés and Ipomedon in the romances of the same name, differ radically from the other participants because they do not wish to compete under their true identity. Unlike the plethora of knights who strive for recognition, Ipomedon and Cligés insist on remaining anonymous and extensively prepare for anonymity. A similar reaction occurs in *Perceval* when Gawain humbly refuses to enter the first day's trials despite the ridicule cast upon him. His refusal is a stark contrast to the eagerness of all the other knights to participate. In the *lais* "Milun" and "Doon," youth and old age are contrasted when the old father competes with the young son. The romances *Partonopeus de Blois* and *La Charrete* provide the contrasts of prisoners competing with freemen, and the *lai* "Guigemar" offers an encounter between the contrasting forces of good and evil.

In discussing the function of the tournament in the works, it is pertinent to examine other purposes it may have that are less thematic in nature than those identified throughout this chapter. Of course, no study of the tournament as a literary device can ignore the remarkable visual effects created through the descriptions of the event. Chrétien de Troyes is perhaps the poet who uses the visual effects to the fullest to portray the beauty of the sport. Using the contest as an area to create aesthetically pleasing images, he emphasizes the colors and designs of the pageant as they appear, for example, in the heraldry; he does not focus on the more brutal and morbid scenes. Without a doubt, other authors create grand visual effects, but they deviate noticeably from Chrétien's style; the author of *Ipomedon* is an example. In this latter romance the visual effects are much more disturbing, and he stresses maiming and carnage rather than pleasing images. Throughout *Ipomedon*, there are passages where saddles are drenched in blood, shields are pierced, chests are split open, and heads are quartered; quite unlike the pictures from a Chrétien romance.

In most of the works, the tournament enhances the sense of adventure for the reader, which is certainly one of the directions of the plot. In other cases, the event produces not heightening of adventure, but a positive feeling after the engagement; in this manner it takes on psychological attributes. In *Amadas et Ydoine*, the fourth tournament enables Amadas to redeem himself: he has learned to talk coherently, to walk and to eat again after his bout with insanity, but he is not completely recovered until he proves himself in a tournament. After the contest, the reader should feel good about what has occurred. In *Perceval*, the tournament also produces a positive emotional effect because Gawain is able to humble the egotistical older sister. Therein, the reader has a sense of satisfaction when the tournament concludes because something good results from the combat, and "bad" does not win. In both "Doon" and "Milun," the emotional effect of the tournament is positive because a father is able to reunite with his son and both are in turn happy.

The psychological effects fostered by a tournament, however, are not always pleasant. In contrast to the narratives with eventual happy endings, in "Chaitivel," "Milun," and *Ipomedon*, the tournament elicits a negative feeling from the reader. In "Milun" and *Ipomedon* this feeling is temporary, giving way to the eventual positive ending and not tainting the rest of the tale; in "Chaitivel" the negativity lingers well to the end. In *Ipomedon*, on the one hand, the overwhelming sense of death at the tournament dampens the spirit of *la Fiere*, as well as of the reader, but on the other, it is accepted by each as a possible consequence of the event.[7] The depressing, negative consequences are eventually eliminated by the rest of the story. The reader continues to follow the saga of Ipomedon after the tournament, and just as he leaves the playing field behind, the reader is able to leave sadness behind. What is remembered at the conclusion of the competition is that Ipomedon was the best knight and by right should obtain the hand of his love. Similarly, the tournament in "Milun" initially creates a negative atmosphere because Milun wants to use it to destroy his adversary whose only fault is his prowess. The reader has an unfavorable opinion of Milun and an unpleasant feeling as the tournament nears. Here too though, the notion is temporary because at the conclusion of the contest, hate has turned to paternal love. Unlike in *Ipomedon* and "Milun" the tournament in "Chaitivel" has permanent negative consequences. The four main male characters are gathered together under means that are not totally honest; three of them later die and the fourth remains forever maimed all due to the activity on the field. At the closure of the tournament, or the *lai* for that matter, there seems to be nothing good that results except for the *lai* itself and the lessons it teaches; the knowledge the lady acquires is good for her but is all the same bitter. The reader has no sense of satisfaction or happiness, just regret and sadness.

Decidedly, tournaments give the poet an excellent opportunity to present vivid passages, be them pleasing or distressing, but they also give the chance to combine all types of activity at once in a fast-paced scene. The rapidity of the tournament is paradoxically often encased in a slow-developing narrative, as seen in *Partonopeus de Blois* where it takes the poet 1378 lines to get from the first indication of the competition to its very start. Once the tournament begins, however, its rapid pace is evidenced by the absence of nutritional breaks. And not once during any of the twenty-seven tournaments in the corpus is there any indication that knights stop to drink or eat. Although they may occasionally rest, and the event may last an entire day, there is no record of nourishment. The omission of repasts is vital to the action because it helps convey the demanding nature of the sport, as well as the physical discipline required to compete.

In conclusion, at first reading, the tournament may appear to be merely a realistic reflection of medieval life or an additional obstacle, another adventure for the hero. Upon closer examination, one realizes the tournament can play a more complex role. While its purposes may overlap at times, it is not included for the same mundane reason. Even if a tournament is merely alluded to or just used in some type of plot pretext, it is significant that it was mentioned at all.

Notes

1. Lucy M. Gay, "Hue de Rotelande's *Ipomedon* and Chrétien de Troyes," in *PMLA* 32 no. 1 (1917): 468–91; 481.

2. Parisse, p. 177.

3. "Le tournoi apparut vite aux chevaliers comme une excellente occasion de prouver leur adresse au combat et d'acquérir une réputation flatteuse." Parisse, p. 183.

4. See chapter on location.

5. I say "supposed" because the author is unknown and could have been male. The characters in the *lai* though, are females and the view presented is supposed to be theirs, not the poet's; this is what I shall assume even though it cannot be proven.

6. Obviously to Ernols, having two non-pagan leaders provides a neutral setting even though two "Christian" leaders, all the same, seem to indicate a marked religious division.

7. One does not have to rejoice at the dead, but as K.G.T. Webster says, "But why object to this sort of thing? Each participant in a tourney knew what he had to expect, and he could generally avoid the worst by running away or surrendering." K.G.T. Webster, "The Twelfth-Century Tourney," in *Anniversary Papers by Colleagues and Pupils of G.L. Kittredge* (Boston: Ginn and Company, 1913), 227–34; 233.

Conclusion

In this endeavor I have isolated numerous aspects and elements of the late-twelfth and early-thirteenth century tournament, outlining them in a comparative and systematic manner. Through the analysis of the works and the respective elements, it is demonstrated that secondary elements, i.e., everything other than procedures and rules, played an important role in the literary tournament. In schematically examining the aspects as they are represented in the literature, it is clear that each time a tournament is alluded to or detailed, it has a purpose or specific role. There is a strategy to it in addition to its being a realistic reflection of medieval life. Of course, it is crucial to the understanding of the early tournament to know why specific weapons were used, and how the sport typically worked, but these are matters already covered by such scholars as Clephan and Barker. This research provides evidence of how the tournament was perceived, presented, and accepted by contemporaneous writers and audiences.

Another task of this investigation has been to determine, if possible, to what extent genre affected the representation of the tournament. I have argued that the question of genre cannot be separated from that of the intended audience. *Le Maréchal* was, no doubt, written to please the son who commissioned it on behalf of his deceased father. Naturally, the poet embellished the virtues of the father, and minimized tragic consequences of his actions, such as the death of any opponents. Understanding why, or more precisely, for whom, *Le Maréchal* was written, helps us to realize that this said work has more literary tendencies than one would believe. By studying *Le Maréchal* in conjunction with contemporary purely fictional narratives, I have illustrated that the latter are sometimes more realistic than the former. This realization does not diminish the value of the narrative, but it suggests that when delving into the tournament, the biographical narrative should be used together with other sources, both literary and iconographical in order to truly fathom its theater.

The tournament in literature develops from, and remains in some ways, analogous to the battle in epic poetry. The elements of the tournament which best ally it with the battles in a *chanson de geste*, e.g., *La Chanson de Roland*, are the graphic bodily injuries, and the militaristic traits found in both types of encounter. Death is also a common denominator of the two, yet viewed differently in a tournament; another element is the motif of national (as it was then perceived) loyalty. It is noticeably a factor in the *chansons de geste* and is a feature in many of the tournament narratives in this study. In *La Chanson de Roland*, Roland and Charlemagne are of French affiliation and battle against mortal enemies, the Saracens—that is, those men ostensibly of Moorish origin. The emphasis therein on nationality is crucial to the plot and epic itself. In "Chaitivel" Marie distinguishes between regional affiliations (generally French and Normand). The biographical narrative, *Le Maréchal*, also frequently distinguishes between regional groups such as *Normanz, Franceis, Engleis*, and *Flamens*. And, although regional ties may be noted in the tournament scenes, there is not as much emphasis on the different allegiances as in the *chansons de geste*, the reason being that the opposing teams in a tournament are not to be viewed as warring factions, hence no need for delineation of nationalistic territories.

The elements of the tournament that affiliate it with the courtly love paradigm are those features that diminish the brutality of the sport and make it more of a pageant than a skirmish. These features are almost always associated with women. And while the early tournament had yet to become mere pageantry as it would in subsequent centuries when ladies would be present, their attendance generates in the knights a strong desire to please and impress. The attention that the knights pay to the women, by carrying sleeves, sashes, and other tokens of love or adoration, helps offset the thoroughly virile aura of the sport. Thus, the tournament acquires traits aligning it more with courtly love episodes than with sporting manifestations.

The treatment of particular aspects of the literary tournament was affected by the genre, the intended audience, and the stance of the Catholic Church. The treatment of casualties is pertinent to the way authors appear to wish to appease the Catholic Church because, although authors consistently use terminology suggestive of injuries, they commonly do not mention any categorically. In fact, most of the time, the audience must simply assume that there are wounds or worse. Even in *Le Maréchal*, the author minimizes the injuries and does not mention any deaths at all. Out of the twenty-seven tournaments in question, only four leave no doubt of combatants' deaths. Surely, the authors purposely avoided reporting numerous casualties in order to counterbalance the Catholic Church's insistence on the dangers of such a competition. In line with this very theme, it has been seen that when the authors are describing the tournament they tend to avoid any mention at all of religion. The one exception occurs in *Partonopeus de Blois* where the poet makes reference to the tourneyers' hearing mass, and briefly differentiates among the combatants as Christian or Pagan.

One finding has served to disprove the notion that early representations of the tournament were not very precise, that the terminology of the sport was vague and confused. According to Coltman Clephan:

> The chroniclers of the joust and tournament of the earlier centuries exhibit a lack of technical knowledge, and the terms they employ are often mixed and conflicting; and, indeed, this confusion continues throughout later centuries also, to an extent making any exact definition of terms extremely difficult.[1]

While Clephan argues that the early works lack a regulated, precise vocabulary for the sport, and the authors show "a lack of technical knowledge," I contend the opposite. The early works, on the contrary, reveal a certain stylized rhetoric of the tournament, borrowing from the military realm as well as the civilian. The one term which did remain in flux and cause confusion was the name assigned to the phenomenon itself. The areas where this confusion appears have been elucidated and the confusion explained.

One aspect not herein treated to any great extent yet which warrants further study, is the allegorical potential that is built into the paradigm of the tournament from its very inception. Several of the tournaments have allegorical implications in their dramatization of the conflict between good and evil. The *lai* "Guigemar" is pertinent in this regard because the hero is invited to a tournament by an evil man. The competition does not take place, but a battle later does in which Guigemar defeats his adversary. The tournament was the original reason for bringing the two forces together and was the field on which the confrontation would have been decided had it actually been held. The tournament in *Ipomedon*, *Perceval*, and "Chaitivel" can also be viewed as representing the conflict between good and evil because in each, a prideful (and, in that sense, evil) woman must be humbled. Unfortunately, innocent people suffer from this pride, and the outcome of "Chaitivel" leaves doubt as to whether the woman is truly humbled. However, the tournament is the focal point at which humility (good) and pride (evil) conflict. The fictional works are more apt to be allegorical representations of these forces than the biographical narrative, but this is natural since, ostensibly, the occurrences in the biography really took place and cannot be readily converted into an abstract play of good and evil.

Because the tournament in medieval literature is such a rich topic, it has been necessary to limit the choices of language, genre, and date. Despite these limitations, the chosen focus area is surely indicative of the whole spectrum of early works in which a tournament might be found. I hope to have illuminated topics heretofore seldom examined, if at all, and that this publication will serve as insight to better understanding the phenomenon called the knightly tournament.

Note

1. Clephan, 9.

Appendix

Tournament Charts

Chart I

Name of Work with beginning line number in text[1]	Indicated Advanced Notice	Knights Attending Mass	Location
Le Maréchal Tour. 1 (v. 1201)	15 days	None	St. James & Valeines, Normandy, France
Tour. 2 (v. 1381)	3 days	None	St. Briz & Boeles, Normandy, France
Tour. 3 (v. 2472)	None	None	Gournei & Ressons, Normandy, France
Tour. 4 (v. 2577)	None	None	Unknown
Tour. 5 (v. 2773)	None	None	Anet & Sorel, Normandy, France
Tour. 6 (v. 2875)	3 weeks	None	Pleurs, Champagne, France
Tour. 7 (v. 3181)	None	None	Eu, Normandy, France
Tour. 8 (v. 3428)	None	None	Joigny, Bourgogne, France
Tour. 9 (v. 3681)	None	None	Maintenon & Nogent, Normandy, France

[1]Beginning line numbers are the first allusions to the particular tournament in question.

Chart I (continued)

Name of Work with beginning line number in text[1]	Indicated Advanced Notice	Knights Attending Mass	Location
Tour. 10 (v. 3888)	None	None	Anet & Sorel (#2)
Tour. 11 (v. 4287)	None	None	Epernon, near Chartres, France
Tour. 12 (v. 4458)	None	None	Lagni sur Marne, Île de France, France
Tour. 13 (v. 4977)	None	None	Epernon (#2)
Tour. 14 (v. 5492)	None	None	Gournei & Ressons (#2)
Tour. 15 (v. 5973)	None	None	Gournei & Ressons (#3)
Tour. 16 (v. 7190)	None	None	St. Pierre sur Dive, Normandy, France
"Guigemar" (v. 744)	None	Did not take place	Brittany, France
"Milun" (v. 385)	None	None	Mont St. Michel, France
"Chaitivel" (v. 73)	None	None	Nantes, France
"Doon" (v. 174)	None	None	Mont St. Michel, France
Erec et Enide (v. 2090)	Approx. 3 weeks	None	Tenebroc, Scotland
La Charrete (v. 5367)	"Long time"	None	Between Pomelgoi & Noauz (England?)
Cligés (v. 4542)	Fortnight	None	Near Oxford & Wallingford, England
Perceval (v. 4805)	None	None	Tintagel, England

Chart I (continued)

Name of Work with beginning line number in text[1]	Indicated Advanced Notice	Knights Attending Mass	Location
Ipomedon (v. 2492)	4 months	None	Catanzaro, Calabria, Italy
Partonopeus de Blois (v. 6547)	1 year	Yes (v. 7865)	Chief d'Oir (France)
Amadas et Ydoine Tour. 1 (v. 843)	None	None	Dijon, France
Tour. 2 (v. 1524)	None	None	Unknown
Tour. 3 (v. 1564)	40 days	Did not take place	Did not take place
Tour. 4 (v. 4076)	8 days	None	Lucca, Italy

Chart II

Name of Work	Women as Spectators[2]	Specific Prizes	Deaths
Le Maréchal Tour. 1	None	None	None
Tour. 2	None	None	None
Tour. 3	None	None	None
Tour. 4	None	None	None
Tour. 5	None	None	None
Tour. 6	Yes, assumed (v. 3042)	Pike (fish) (v. 3047)	None
Tour. 7	None	None	None
Tour. 8	Yes (v. 3524)	None	None
Tour. 9	None	None	None
Tour. 10	None	None	None
Tour. 11	None	None	None
Tour. 12	None	None	None
Tour. 13	None	None	None
Tour. 14	None	None	None
Tour. 15	None	None	None
Tour. 16	None	None	None

[2]The verse line given for this category is approximately the first indication that women are, or are to be, present. In some instances (e.g., *Ipomedon*), women appear too frequently to pinpoint. Othertimes (e.g., *Amadas et Ydoine*), the given line is the only reference to their presence.

Chart II (continued)

Name of Work	Women as Spectators[2]	Specific Prizes	Deaths
"Guigemar"	Did not take place	Did not take place	Did not take place
"Milun"	None	None	None
"Chaitivel"	Yes (v. 107)	The Lady's love	3 knights
"Doon"	None	None	None
Erec et Enide	Yes, assumed	None	None
La Charrete	Yes (v. 5582)	Maidens as Spouses	None
Cligés	None	None	None
Perceval	Yes (v. 4926)	Maiden's hand in marriage is assumed	None
Ipomedon	Yes (v. 3604)	Princess' hand in marriage	Numerous
Partonopeus de Blois	Yes (v. 7877)	Princess' hand in marriage	Numerous
Amadas et Ydoine Tour. 1	Yes (v. 856)	None	None
Tour. 2	Unknown	Unknown	Unknown
Tour. 3	Did not take place	Did not take place	Did not take place
Tour. 4	None	None	Numerous

Chart III

Name of Work	Duration	Number of Participants
Le Maréchal Tour. 1	1 day	More than 40
Tour. 2	1 day	9 specifically identified, but no other number
Tour. 3	1 day	"Many" but no other number
Tour. 4	1 day	"Many" but no other number
Tour. 5	1 day	More than 300
Tour. 6	1 day	"So many the ground resembled ants" but no number
Tour. 7	1 day	More than 100
Tour. 8	1 day	No number
Tour. 9	1 day	No number
Tour. 10	1 day	27 specifically identified, but no other number
Tour. 11	1 day	No number
Tour. 12	1 day	Over 3000
Tour. 13	1 day	"Many" but 7 specifically identified
Tour. 14	1 day	"Many" but no other number
Tour. 15	1 day	"Many" but 39 specifically identified
Tour. 16	1 day	No number

Chart III (continued)

Name of Work	Duration	Number of Participants
"Guigemar"	Did not take place	Over 100 were expected
"Milun"	1 day	No number
"Chaitivel"	1 day	Over 2000
"Doon"	1 day	No number
Erec et Enide	2 days	11 specifically identified, but no other number
La Charrete	2 days	Over 415
Cligés	4 days	"Many" but 6 specifically identified
Perceval	2 days	"Many" but no number
Ipomedon	3 days	Over 1510
Partonopeus de Blois	3 days	"By the thousands"
Amadas et Ydoine Tour. 1	1 day	Over 100
Tour. 2	Unknown	Unknown
Tour. 3	Did not take place	Did not take place
Tour. 4	1 day	Over 40

Bibliography

Primary Sources

Ambroise. *L'Estoire de la guerre sainte: histoire en vers de la troisième croisade*. Edited by Gaston Paris. Paris: Imprimerie Nationale, 1897.

Chrétien de Troyes. *Erec et Enide*. Translated by Carleton Carroll. New York and London: Garland Publishing, 1987.

———. *Les Romans de Chrétien de Troyes: Cligés*. Edited by Alexandre Micha. Vol. 2 of 6 vols. Paris: Librairie Ancienne Honoré Champion, 1957.

———. *Les Romans de Chrétien de Troyes: Le Chevalier de la charrete*. Edited by Mario Roques. Vol. 3 of 6 vols. Paris: Librairie Ancienne Honoré Champion, 1958.

———. *Les Romans de Chrétien de Troyes: Le Conte du Graal*. Edited by Felix Lecoy. Vols. 1 and 2 of 6 vols. Paris: Honoré Champion, 1973 and 1975.

———. *Yvain, Le Chevalier au lion*. Translated by William Kibler. New York and London: Garland Publishing, 1985.

Crapelet, G.-A., ed. *Partonopeus de Blois*. Paris: L'Imprimerie de Crapelet, 1834.

Hue de Rotelande. *Ipomedon*. Edited by A. J. Holden. Paris: Klincksieck, 1979.

Huon d'Oisi. "Le Tournoiement des dames." In *La Poésie lyrique d'Oïl*, eds. I. M. Cluzel and L. Pressouyre, 37–45. Paris: A. G. Nizet, 1969.

Lambert, Curé d'Ardre. *Chronique de Guines et D'Ardre*. Paris: Jules Renouard, 1855.

Marie de France. *Les Lais de Marie de France*. Edited by Jean Rychner. Paris: Honoré Champion, 1968.

Meyer, Paul, ed. *L'Histoire de Guillaume le Maréchal*. 3 vols. Paris: Reynouard, 1891.

Normand, Jacques, and Gaston Raynaud, eds. *Aiol*. Paris: Librairie de Firmin Didot et Cie., 1877.

Paris, Gaston. "Les Lais Inédits de Tyolet, de Guingamor, de Doon, du Lecheor et de Tydorel." *Romania* 8 no. 1 (1879): 29–72.

Raynaud de Lage, Guy, ed. *Le Roman de Thèbes*. 2 vols. Paris: Honoré Champion, 1968.

Reinhard, John R., ed. *Amadas et Ydoine*. Paris: Librairie Ancienne Honoré Champion, 1926.

René d'Anjou. *Traité de la forme et devis d'un tournoi*. Edited by Edmond Pognon. Paris: Verve, 1946.

Salverda de Grave, J-J., ed. *Enéas - Roman du XIIe siècle*. 2 vols. Paris: Honoré Champion, 1964.

Smedt, Charles de, ed. *Gesta Pontificum Cameracensium: Gestes des Evêques de Cambrai de 1092 à 1138—Gesta Nicolai*. La Société de l'histoire par (lui). Paris: Libraire Renouard, 1880.

Secondary Sources

Aubailly, Jean-Claude, trans. *Amadas et Ydoine*. Paris: Honoré Champion, 1986.

Auerbach, Erich. *Mimesis: The Representation of Reality in Western Literature*. Translated by William Trask. Princeton: Princeton University Press, 1968.

Barber, Richard. *The Knight and Chivalry*. Ipswich: The Boydell Press, 1974.

Barker, Juliet. *The Tournament in England 1100–1400*. Suffolk: St. Edmundsbury Press, 1986.

Barker, Juliet, and Maurice Keen. "The Medieval English Kings and the Tournament." In *Das ritterliche Turnier im Mitterlalter*, ed. Josef Fleckenstein, 212–228. Göttingen: Vandenhœck & Ruprecht, 1985.

Bec, Pierre, ed. "La Bele Doete." In *La Lyrique Française au moyen âge*. Vol. 2 of 2 vols. Paris: Editions A. & J. Picard, 1978; 33–35.

Bell, Andrew. *A History of Feudalism British and Continental.* London: Longman, Green, Longman, Roberts, & Green, 1863.

Bloch, Marc. *Feudal Society.* Translated by L. A. Manyon. Chicago: University of Chicago Press, 1962.

Bloch, Oscar, and W. von Wartburg. *Dictionnaire étymologique de la langue française.* Paris: Presses Universitaires de France, 1964.

Bossuat, Robert. *Le Moyen Age.* Paris: J. De Gigord, 1931.

Bumke, Joachim. *The Concept of Knighthood in the Middle Ages.* Translated by W.T.H., and Eriks Jackson. New York: AMS Press, 1982.

Chênerie, Marie-Luce. ""Ces curieux chevaliers tournoyeurs . . ." des fabliaux aux romans" *Romania* 97 no. 3 (1976): 327–368.

————. *Le Chevalier errant dans les romans arthuriens en vers des XIIe et XIIIe siècles.* Genève: Droz, 1986.

Clephan, Coltman R. *The Tournament, Its Periods and Phases.* New York: Frederick Ungar, 1919.

Cline, Ruth Huff. "Tournaments of English and French Literature Compared with Those of History, 1100–1500." Ph. D. diss., University of Chicago, 1939.

Comfort, W. W. *Arthurian Romances.* London: Dent, 1968.

Cowling, Samuel T. "The Image of the Tournament in Marie de France's *Le Chaitivel.*" *Romance Notes* 16 no. 3 (spring 1975): 686–691.

Cripps-Day, Francis Henry. *The History of the Tournament in England and France.* London: B. Quaritch, 1918.

Daniel-Rops, H. *Cathedral and Crusade*. Translated by John Warrington. London: J. M. Dent & Sons, Ltd., 1957.

Denholm-Young, Noël. "The Tournament in the Thirteenth Century." In *Studies in Medieval History Presented to Frederick Maurice Powicke*, eds., R. W. Hunt, W. A. Pantin and R. W. Southern, 240–268. Oxford: The Clarendon Press, 1948.

Duby, Georges. *The Chivalrous Society*. Translated by Cynthia Postan. London: Edward Arnold, 1977.

————. *William Marshal: The Flower of Chivalry*. Translated by Richard Howard. New York: Pantheon, 1985.

————. *The Legend of Bouvines*. Translated by Catherine Tihanyi. Cambridge: Polity Press, 1990.

Duby, Georges, and R. Mandrou. *Moyen Age—XVIe siècle*. Vol. 1, *Histoire de la civilisation française*. Paris: Armand Colin, 1958.

Ferrante, Joan. *Woman as Image in Medieval Literature*. New York: Columbia University Press, 1975.

Flutre, Louis-Fernand. *Table des noms propres avec toutes leurs variantes figurant dans les romans du Moyen Age écrits en français ou en provençal et actuellement publiés ou analysés*. Poitiers: Centre d'Etudes Supérieures de civilisation médiévale, 1962.

Gautier, Léon, ed. *La Chanson de Roland*. 13th ed. Tours: Alfred Mame et fils, 1883.

Gay, Lucy M. "Hue de Rotelande's *Ipomedon* and Chrétien de Troyes." *PMLA* 32 no. 1 (1917): 468–491.

Gies, Frances. *The Knight in History*. New York: Harper and Row, 1984.

Gies, Joseph, and Frances. *Life in a Medieval Castle*. New York: Harper and Row, 1974.

————. *Life in a Medieval City*. New York: Harper and Row, 1969.

Godefroy, Frédéric. *Dictionnaire de l'ancienne langue française et de tous les dialectes du IXe au XVe siècle*. Paris: F. Vieweg, 1885.

Golinsky, Marie-Françoise, and Alice Vidal. *The Love of France*. London: Octopus Books Limited, 1977.

Greimas, A. J., ed. *Larousse Trésors du français—Dictionnaire de l'ancien français: Le Moyen âge*. Paris: Larousse, 1994.

Hanning, Robert, and Joan Ferrante, trans. *The Lais of Marie de France*. New York: Dutton, 1978.

Harper-Bill, Christopher, and Ruth Harvey. *The Ideals and Practice of Medieval Knighthood*. Suffolk: Boydell Press, 1986.

Hatzfeld, Adolphe, Arsène Darmesteter, and Antoine Thomas, eds., *Dictionnaire Général de la langue française*. Paris: Librairie Delagrave, 1920.

Hopkins, Andrea. *Knights*. New York: Artabas, 1990.

Hovedon, Roger de. *Chronica Magistri Rogeri de Houedene*. Edited by William Stubbs. Parts 1–4, vol. 51 of *Rerum Brittannicarum Medii Ævi Scriptores*, 102 vols. London: Longman and Trübner, 1870.

Howlett, Richard, ed. *Historia Rerum Anglicarum*, part 2, vol. 82 of *Rerum Brittannicarum Medii Ævi Scriptores*, 102 vols. London: Longman & Co., 1885.

Jusserand, J. J. "Les Sports dans l'ancienne France." *Revue de Paris*. No. 10 (Mai 1900): 288–327.

Kibler, William W., trans. *Lancelot or, The Knight of the Cart (Le Chevalier de la charrete)*. New York and London: Garland Publishing, 1981.

Köhler, Erich. *L'Aventure chevaleresque*. Translated by Elaine Kaufholz. Paris: Gallimard, 1974.

Lacroix, Paul. *Military and Religious Life in the Middle Ages and the Renaissance*. New York: Frederick Ungar, 1964.

Lavisse, Ernest. *Histoire de France: Depuis les origines jusqu'à la révolution. Tome troisième: Louis VII—Philippe-Auguste—Louis VIII (1137–1226)*. Ed. by Achille Luchaire. Paris: Librairie Hachette et Cie., 1911.

LeGoff, Jacques. *Time, Work, and Culture in the Middle Ages*. Translated by Arthur Goldhammer. Chicago: University of Chicago Press, 1980.

————. "Réalités sociales et codes idéologiques au début du XIIIe siècle: un exemplun de Jacques de Vitry sur les tournois." In L'Imaginaire médiéval: essais, 248–61. Paris: Gallimard, 1985.

Lock, Richard. Aspects of Time in Medieval Literature. New York: Garland Publishing, Inc., 1985.

Ménard, Philippe. "Les Vespres del tournoiement." In Miscellanea di Studi Romanzi offerta a Guiliano Gasca Querirazza per suo 65o compleanno, 651–662. Torino: Edizioni Dell'Orso, 1988.

Meyer, Paul. "L'Histoire de Guillaume le Maréchal." Romania 11 no. 1 (1882): 22–74.

Mölk, Ulrich. "Remarques philologiques sur tornoi(ement) dans la littérature française des XIIe et XIIIe siècles." In Badia I Margarit. Symposium in Honorem Prof. M. de Riquer, 277–87. Barcelona: Universitat de Barcelona, 1986.

Moorman, Charles, and Ruth. An Arthurian Dictionary. Jackson: University of Jackson Press of Mississippi, 1978.

Munro, Dana Carleton. The Middle Ages: 395–1272. 7 vols. New York: The Century Co., 1921.

Norden, Ernest E. "The Figure of the Father in the Romances of Chrétien de Troyes." South Central Bulletin 37 no. 4 (Winter 1978): 155–57.

Otaka, Yorio. "Vocabulaire du combat dans les lais de Marie de France." In VIII Congreso de la Société Rencevalls: Pamplona-Santiago de Compostela, 15 a 25 de agosto de 1978, 367–73. Pamplona: Institutión Principe de Viana, 1981.

Ott, André G. Etude sur les couleurs en vieux français. Paris: Librairie Emile Bouillon, 1899.

Painter, Sidney. French Chivalry: Chivalric Ideas and Practices in Mediæval France. Baltimore: The John Hopkins Press, 1940.

————. William Marshal: Knight-Errant, Baron, and Regent of England. Baltimore: The John Hopkins Press, 1933.

Paris, Gaston. "Sur Amadas et Idoine." In Mélanges de littérature française, 328–36. Paris: 1912.

Parisse, Michel. "Le tournoi en France des origines à la fin du XIIIe siècle." In *Das ritterliche Turnier im Mitterlalter*, ed. Josef Fleckenstein, 175–211. Göttingen: Vandenhœck & Ruprecht, 1985.

Pastoureau, Michel. *La Vie quotidienne en France et en Angleterre au temps des chevaliers de la table ronde (XIIe–XIIIe siècles)*. Paris: Hachette, 1976.

Pauphilet, Albert, ed. *Historiens et chroniqueurs du moyen âge*. Paris: Gallimard, 1963.

Picherit, Jean-Louis. "Le Motif du tournoi dont le prix est la main d'une riche et noble héritière." *Romance Quarterly* 36 no. 2 (May 1989): 141–52.

Poe, Elizabeth Wilson. "The Problem of the Tournament in *Chaitivel*." In *In Quest of Marie de France: A Twelfth-Century Poet*, ed. Chantal Maréchal, 175–192. Lewiston, New York: Edwin Mellen Press, 1992.

Pollack, Jodi. "Images in Time in Chrétien de Troyes's *Lancelot*, *Perceval* and *Yvain*." Senior Honor's Thesis, Tulane University, 1990.

Powicke, Sir Frederick Maurice. *King Henry III and the Lord Edward*. 2 vols. Oxford: Clarendon Press, 1947.

———. *Medieval England 1066–1485*. London: Thornton, Butterworth, 1931.

———. *The Loss of Normandy 1189–1204*. Manchester: The University Press, 1960.

———. *Ways of Medieval Life and Thought*. London: Odhams Press, 1955.

Powicke, Michael. *Military Obligation in Medieval England*. Oxford: Clarendon Press, 1962.

Ribard, Jacques. *Le moyen âge: Littérature et symbolisme*. Geneva: Editions Slatkine, 1984.

Richardson, H. G., and G. O. Sayles. *The Governance of Mediæval England*. Edinburgh: Edinburgh University Press, 1963.

Rothwell, W. "The Hours of the Day in Medieval French." *French Studies* 13 no. 3 (July 1959): 240–51.

Stanesco, Michael. *Jeux d'errance du chevalier médiéval*. Leiden: E. J. Brill, 1988.

Stephenson, Carl. *Medieval History*. 3rd ed. New York: Harper & Brothers, 1951.

Strutt, Joseph. *Sports and Pastimes of the People of England*. London: Methusen & Co., 1801.

Stubbs, William, ed. *Chronicles and Memorials of the Reign of Richard I*, part 1, vol. 38 of *Rerum Brittannicarum Medii Ævi Scriptores*, 102 vols. London: Longman, Green, Longman, Roberts, and Green, 1864.

————. ed. *Select Charters and Other Illustrations of English Constitutional History*. 8th Edition. Oxford: Clarendon Press, 1895.

Thomson, Richard. *An Historical Essay on the Magna Charta of King John*. London: The Apollo Press, 1829.

Turner, Ralph V. *The King and His Courts*. New York: Cornell University Press, 1968.

Vale, Malcolm. *War and Chivalry*. London: Duckworth and Co., 1981.

Wagner, Anthony Edward. *Heralds and Heraldry in the Middle Ages*. London: Oxford University Press, 1939.

Webster, K. G. T. "The Twelfth-Century Tourney." In *Anniversary Papers by Colleagues and Pupils of G. L. Kittredge*. 227–234. Boston: Ginn and Company, 1913.

West, C. B. *Courtoisie in Anglo-Normand Literature*. New York: Haskell House, 1966.

West, G. D. *An Index of Proper Names in French Arthurian Romances 1150-1300*. Toronto: University of Toronto Press, 1969.

Weston, Jessie L. *The Three Days' Tournament*. New York: Haskell House, 1965.

Winters, Dorothy. "The Three Days' Combat." Ph. D. diss., University of Chicago, 1931.

Index

Studies in the Humanities

Edited by Guy Mermier

The Studies in the Humanities series welcomes manuscripts discussing various aspects of the humanities. The series' emphasis is on medieval and Renaissance literatures with a focus on Western civilizations and cultures. Submissions dealing with linguistics, history, politics, or sociology within the same time frame and geographical bounds are also encouraged. Manuscripts may be submitted in English, French, or Italian. The preferred style manual is the MLA Handbook (1995).

For additional information about this series or for the submission of manuscripts, please contact:

Peter Lang Publishing, Inc.
Acquisitions Department
516 N. Charles St., 2nd Floor
Baltimore, MD 21201

To order other books in this series, please contact our Customer Service Department at:

800-770-LANG (within the U.S.)
(212) 647-7706 (outside the U.S.)
(212) 647-7707 FAX

or browse online by series at:

www.peterlang.com